UNLOCKING
THE SECRETS
of being

loved,
accepted
&secure

UNLOCKING
THE SECRETS
of being

loved, accepted & secure

Josh McDowell
& Dale Bellis

WORD PUBLISHING
Dallas · London · Sydney · Singapore

Library of Congress Cataloging in Publication Data

McDowell, Josh.
    Evidence for joy.
    Bibliography: p.
    1. Christian life—1960- . 2. Faith. 3. Apologetics—20th
century. I. Bellis, Dale E., 1951- . II. Title
    BV4501.2.M4355 1984 248.4   84-11900

ISBN 0-8499-0400-5
ISBN 0-8499-2978-4 (pbk.)
ISBN 0-8499-3171-1 (condensed pbk.)

9 8 9 0 1 2 3 AGF 9 8 7 6 5 4 3 2 1

Printed in the United States of America

Contents

1

Searching in All the Wrong Places

You and I, as human beings, long for a lasting intimate love relationship where we can feel unconditionally accepted and secure. We were created by God with that longing, a longing He wants to fulfill. Yet many have not understood God's design to satisfy those needs, and end up searching for love, acceptance, and security in all the wrong places—even in places that seem to be legitimate.

A young lady wrote me recently and stated a condition I find many people identifying with today:

> Dear Mr. McDowell,
>
> I wish someone would just love me, and I don't mean physically. I want someone to show me that he cares. . . . I want to be loved, but I don't know how to accept or give love.

Not long ago I was invited to Louisiana State University to deliver a three-night lecture series. During the day I spoke at the open air meeting. Louisiana State still has a "free speech" platform, popular during the student unrest days of the late sixties. From three to five on Wednesday afternoon everything stops. At a designated spot, nine speakers have ten minutes each to say anything they want. I spoke seventh in line. As I stepped to the platform, hundreds of students milled on the grass. Some were reading; others were tossing a football or throwing Frisbees. In some cases, students yelled and screamed at speakers. In general, they paid no attention!

I stared at the crowd for a moment, and then said loudly, "Most of you here struggle with two fears."

In a matter of seconds, it was as if a "silence bomb" had hit the place. Everyone quieted. I couldn't believe it! Minutes before they had shouted, jeered, and heckled each speaker. Now, everyone listened.

I continued, "One, you have the fear that you will never be loved, and, two, the fear that you will never be able to love."

Absolute silence. Stares. They knew it was true.

But those nagging doubts about our ability to love and be loved are not our only problem. Let's be honest. Do you really like the person you are? If you do, count yourself fortunate. Most of us are suffering from a low self-image. And this is true regardless of the many excellent books addressing this need. Practical resources bursting with biblically sound teaching on personal acceptance and how to develop a positive self-image crowd Christians' shelves. Yet how much has your self-concept really been helped by these resources?

Psychology tells us that the way you view yourself is one of the hardest things for you to change. So many long to be at ease with themselves, to accept themselves, and they really try. But most of their attempts fail. One reason for this is that behind much of the disintegration of an individual's self-concept is another problem—a deep sense of insecurity, an inability to face life's crises with confidence and assurance. A deep vacuum of uncertainty fills many lives. Possessions, people, or power are some of the straws grasped to fill that void. Nothing seems to work. The pain persists.

Yet you and I can know we are truly loved, accepted, and secure in a world of lost love, self-doubt, and uncertainty. How? I believe the answer is foundationally in a personal faith relationship in Jesus Christ. Notice, I didn't say the answer was in religion or church or even in faith itself—I said a personal faith relationship *in* Jesus Christ. And if you'll bear with me, I believe that I can explain how you can unlock the secrets of being loved, accepted, and secure through a dynamic faith relationship in Christ. But before I share that, let me tell you about . . .

MY SEARCH

Tragically, I stumbled through life for years not trusting God personally. So my deepest longings for love, acceptance, and security went unfulfilled. As a non-Christian at Kellogg College, my goal in life was to be one of the happiest individuals in the entire world. Thomas Aquinas wrote: "There is within every soul a thirst for happiness and meaning." I wanted answers to questions: "Who am I?" "What am I?" "Why in the world am I here?" "Where am I going?" I wanted to be loved; I wanted to be accepted; I wanted to face life with confidence and security. And during my college years I set out on a search to discover the truth about life, about religion, about Christianity. I was empty inside. I wanted purpose in life.

When I remember my childhood growing up on a 150-acre dairy farm near Union City, Michigan, the happy times that come to mind are when I went fishing with my friend Dave in the creek that ran by our house or boating with my uncle on Rose Lake. But the childhood memories most vivid in my mind are the ego-shattering experiences which were part of my everyday existence.

I am naturally left-handed, but as a grade-school child I was forced by my teachers to change from being left-handed to being right-handed. One teacher, Mrs. Duel, stood over me with a ruler to slap my left hand if I reached out for anything with it. "Think, Josh," she would say. "Use your right hand!" I came to believe that left-handedness was inferior to right-handedness, and therefore I was inferior. As a result of my feelings of inferiority and the nervousness created by such treatment, I developed a speech impediment. My poor self-image and low self-esteem were compounded by my inability to speak properly. Not only did I feel clumsy and inadequate, but now stupid as well as I struggled to speak in front of my peers when called on in class.

Even some of my friends seemed to be as insecure and unable to succeed as I was. I recall a red-headed firebreather named Jerry who lived near our two-story wood frame farmhouse. Anything could make Jerry mad. His patience was very thin. Jerry would try to help his dad with the work around the house, and on many occasions his dad would say, "Jerry, you can't do anything right!" It did seem to be true. Jerry would try and put a screw in a hole, and if it didn't go in the first time he would lose his temper, jam the screw, and strip the threads. Then it would never work, which made him madder. I remember building a "fort" together with Jerry in the woods behind our house. We imagined it to be our last defense against marauding savages and we were the last hope of protection for the civilized world. We had to build our fort fast! In his fury, if a pole wouldn't fit, or a nail bent, Jerry would yell, "I can't do anything right!" Jerry grew up believing he was what his dad thought of him—an incompetent, mistake-prone clod. What child wouldn't believe his mom and dad? Or his teacher? Who else can he trust? Needless to say, Jerry and I never finished the fort.

And yet, these painful memories do not compare with the devastation caused in my life by my father. To me he was the town alcoholic. Union City is a small town of several thousand people. Everyone knew everyone else, and everyone knew my father. My friends in high school made jokes about him. They didn't think it bothered me. I laughed on the outside, but cried on the inside. Sometimes I'd go out in the barn and see my mother lying in the manure behind the cows, beaten so badly she couldn't get up. How I hated my father for his cruelty to her! The only sense of security and stability I had as a child came from my mother's constant love. No matter where I had been or how early or late I came home, my mother always seemed to be there waiting for me. To vent my anger against my father and to avenge his mistreatment of my mother, I would try to humiliate him. If I knew my friends would be coming to the house, if my father was drunk, I would tie him up in the barn and park the car up around the silo. I would tell my friends he was gone. I don't think anyone could have hated anyone more than I hated him.

The emotional insecurity and turmoil of my high school years set the stage for the search for meaning in my life I was to undertake during college. Although the big questions were as yet unarticulated in my mind, I was emotionally and spiritually bankrupt. I longed to be loved with an unconditional, unstoppable love. I wanted to be accepted by others, but more than this, I needed to be able to accept myself, to overcome my feelings of self-hatred. I wanted security, that sense of confidence that would allow me to live life with a peaceful heart and mind.

As high school graduation neared I looked forward to the freedom I would experience at college. No longer would there be the stigma of being the son of the town drunk. I could be a new person, my own person. I would find meaning for my life and, above all, happiness. When I began to look around me, it seemed that the most likely place to turn for answers was religion. Almost everyone I knew was into some sort of "religion," so I did the obvious thing and went to church. I went in the morning, I went in the afternoon, and I went in the evening. But there was no joy for me in church. I felt worse inside the church than I did outside. All the while, I focused my attention on *my* efforts. As a result, my "believing" became performance based. I thought approval could be won from God and others by my piety. But what a disappointment. "Religion" was clearly not the answer I was looking for.

During my freshman year at college I began to wonder if the answers to my need for being loved, accepted, and secure were in prestige. Becoming a leader, giving myself to a "cause," and being known on campus might possibly be the route to happiness. At college the student government leaders held the purse strings and threw their weight around. It seemed to me an attractive position to be in, so I ran for freshman class president and was elected. My ego was boosted by knowing everyone on campus and hearing, "Hi, Josh," from others. It was great making important decisions such as choosing which outside speakers to invite to campus; I spent the university's and the students' money to get the speakers I wanted. I threw more parties with student money than anyone else. But my happiness, like the happiness of so many others, depended upon my own circumstances. If things were going great, I felt great. When things would go lousy, I felt lousy. I would wake up Monday morning, usually with a headache from the activities of the night before, and my attitude was, "Well, here go another five days." I endured the routine of Monday through Friday, but happiness revolved around three nights a week: Friday, Saturday, and Sunday. Then the vicious cycle would begin all over again.

But there didn't seem to be anyone living any differently, or anyone who could tell me how to change the path of my downward spiral into despair and bitterness. Despite great frustration, there was a sincerity in my search for answers to life's important questions: "Who am I?" "Why am I here?" "Where am I going?"

As weeks went by, I began to notice on campus a small group of people: eight students and two faculty members. There was something different about their lives. They seemed to know why they believed what they believed. I enjoy being around people like that. Whether I agree with them or not, I admire a man or woman with conviction. The people in this small group seemed to know where they were going. That's unusual among many university students. I noticed that more than just talking about love, they went out of their way to help others. Their happiness was not dependent on circumstances; rather, they seemed to rise above flat bicycle tires, tough exams, demanding professors, lost football tickets, and rude dorm mates. They had an inner source of constant joy, love, and security. They had something I didn't have.

Like the average student, when somebody had something I didn't have, I wanted it. So, I decided to make friends with these intriguing people.

Two weeks later we were all sitting around a table in the student union. After a few moments of casual conversation, one student mentioned God. Now let's face it, if you're an insecure person, and a conversation centers on God, you tend to get a little uneasy and try to put on a big front. Every campus, business office, or community has a big mouth, a person who says, "Aw, come on. . . . Christianity, ha! That's for the weaklings; it's not intellectual."

Well, I put on the "big front." I looked over at one of the students, nonchalantly leaned back in my chair, and said, "Tell me, what changed your lives? Why are your lives so different from those of the other students, the leaders on campus, the professors?"

That young woman looked me straight in the eye and said two words I never thought I'd hear uttered with respect at that university. She said, "Jesus Christ." I said, "Oh, for heaven's sake, don't give me that garbage. I'm fed up with religion; I'm fed up with the church; I'm fed up with the Bible. Don't give me that garbage about religion." She shot back, "Mister, I didn't say religion; I said Jesus Christ."

I apologized for my attitude, and then they challenged me intellectually to examine the claim that Jesus Christ is God's Son; that taking on human flesh, He lived among real men and women and died on the cross for the sins of mankind; that He was buried and He arose three days later; and that He could change a person's life in the twentieth century.

These people challenged me again and again. Finally I accepted their challenge, but out of the wrong motive. Rather than desiring to learn the truth about Christianity, I wanted to refute its claims. I didn't know there were undeniable facts; I didn't know there was evidence to be evaluated; I didn't know there were reasons why I could know for certain that I was loved, accepted, and secure.

So, I set out to intellectually refute Christianity. After two years of research, the whole plan backfired on me. The evidence I uncovered convinced me Jesus Christ *was* who He claimed to be—the Son of God, the Savior of the world. After an intense personal struggle, I committed my life to Christ. And for the past twenty-five years I have been sharing the joy of that love relationship with all who would listen.

Christ changed my life. When I trusted Christ as Savior, I received the love, acceptance, and security I had sought for so long. Where there was hatred He gave love. Where there was rejection He gave acceptance. Where there was insecurity He gave security. Through my search for faith in Christ I found an intelligent basis on which to have my deepest needs fully met.

THE REAL PROBLEM

Christ can be trusted to keep His Word that He will exchange our drab existence for joyous, abundant living! And while true love, total acceptance, and complete security are rare in our frantic world, the biblical evidence that our desires in these areas will be fulfilled in Christ is abundant.

Then what's the problem? Why are people's needs not fully met in these areas? It is because so many do not understand the basis for our faith in Christ to meet these deep needs.

Faith is the key. Faith is at the root of appropriating those spiritual blessings you already have in Christ. Faith seizes and makes experiential what is already yours in Christ potentially. Faith brings down to earth in actuality what is true of you in the heavenlies (Eph. 1:3). Faith meets you where you are with your hurts, frustrations, and even anguish.

Do you want a confident assurance you will always be loved and be able to love? Know why you believe God will always love you. Do you want assurance you will always be accepted? Know why you believe God finds you acceptable. Do you want confidence you will always be secure? Know why you believe God will always fulfill His promises. Knowing why you believe is the secret to a fulfilled and joyful life. Knowing *why* you believe will enable you to lay claim to the love, acceptance, and security God already has for you.

But is it really that simple? Simple, yes. Easy? No. Life serves up many reasons to doubt that you're loved, accepted, and secure. Life with all its trials may bring you face to face with the stark reality that you are not loved by those around you. Can you still feel loved even during the tragedy of a lost love? You can if you know why you believe God loves you.

It's not too hard to feel accepted when friends are kind and loving. But what happens when you're falsely accused or unjustly mistreated? Can you still feel accepted when you're facing the cruel rejection of others? You can if you know why you believe God accepts you.

When all is calm and serene, it's not difficult to feel safe and secure. But when you fail a course in school, lose a job, face mounting debts, or stand numbly gazing upon the lifeless body of a loved one—what then? Can you still have confidence, assurance, and security when the walls of life come crashing in on you? You can if you know why you believe God is your security.

In fact, life with all its trials and difficulties is the very place God wishes to demonstrate His faithfulness to you. He wants you to know why you can believe Him to be your source of being loved, accepted, and secure. He wants to teach you how your faith can appropriate all the love, acceptance, and security you will ever need. Let's go on to learn how.

2

A Case for Lost Love

I strolled through the student union past the common television parlor. The room was packed with every occupant intently absorbed in a program. I slipped inside to see what was of such interest.

"Believe me, Genesta, I love *you*—you've got to believe me." With head down, the actress softly asked, "But what about your wife?" The handsome doctor lifted Genesta's head tenderly and gazed passionately into her eyes. "Genesta, you are the only one who means anything to me any more. You've got to believe that."

A girl in the room broke the silence and absorption of the crowd as she blurted out: "If you believe him, Genesta, you're crazy." The crowd chuckled as the organ music swelled, the credits rolled, and the teaser for the next episode faded out.

That's par for the course for most daytime soap operas. But the television dialogue reminded me once again of the relationship between faith and love: *"Believe* me, I love *you*— you've got to *believe* me."

A significant step in getting our love needs met and developing the freedom to return love is discovering the relationship between our faith in Christ and our need to love and be loved. There was a time, before coming to Christ, when I didn't see a relationship between faith and love. Tragically, even many *Christians* are blind to this truth. Faith for them becomes a part of a person's spiritual life exercised in prayer and worship and unconnected to loving and feeling loved; they separate faith from facts, practical matters from spiritual ones. Faith influences our communion with God—it's only spiritual, they think. Loving and being loved affects our personal relationships—it's practical, unrelated to matters of faith. How wrong!

Faith was never meant to be merely a "spiritual" exercise that rarely touches our practical needs. Our love relationship with Christ is designed to teach every husband and wife, or parent and child, exciting insights for an abiding love for one another. I see a definite and vital connection between faith in Christ and the ability to give and receive love. The challenge is to take what you know about God's love through faith and appropriate it in such a way that your emotions and those of the ones you love are transformed.

Let's look at the story of a real-life couple to see this process in action.

KAREN AND DAN

My wife and I greeted Karen warmly as she came off the plane. We had known Karen and her husband, Dan, for over eight years. We had lived near Karen and Dan in Dallas during my early ministry. Visiting together often, we soon became fast friends. Dan was from southern Missouri, and Karen from Kansas. They had met as teenagers, and their friendship soon blossomed into romance, and romance into marriage. Dan worked long hours as a building contractor. They didn't have any children.

Now their marriage had run into trouble, and Karen had come for help. She said she had to get away and try to get her feelings sorted out. During the hour drive from the airport, Karen confessed her long, bitter story.

"All our married life I've had a hidden fear our marriage would break up," she said. "And now my nightmare has come true. It's not that I hate Dan for what's happened. I'm trying to forgive him. But I can't get over the feeling that Dan never did love me." Her head dropped. She broke into tears. "You know, you think you're close to someone; you think they really love you, and then you realize they don't love you. It's really painful. I know this other woman doesn't mean anything to Dan. He says he loves me, but right now, I don't know if I can ever love Dan, or any man, again."

Karen gave us a brief chronology of the breakdown of their relationship. The first crack appeared as a result of their social life. Their calendar, under Dan's command, was booked solid. Dan was a very likable person; he had a good sense of humor and knew how to make people laugh. And he genuinely enjoyed being with people. Karen wanted a more quiet life, though, time just to be together at home. But Dan insisted he needed the outside fellowship and friendship.

"It's gotten to the place I simply don't care if we go anywhere any more," Karen told us, riding back from the airport. "It wouldn't be so bad if I could just feel comfortable around his friends. But, honestly, I feel alone in those crowds. I'm always watching Dan talk to everyone else; he acts as though I don't exist. And the reasons why are pretty obvious when he focuses 90 percent of his attention on two or three women the entire evening."

"Did you talk to Dan about your feelings?" we asked.

"Yes," she said. "I talked to him, and he said I was jealous. He said those girls meant nothing to him, and he was just being sociable."

Some months after their confrontation, as Karen recounted, another troubling sign appeared. Dan occasionally called one of the women of the church from work. They were on a church committee together and needed to discuss the details of a project, Dan explained. Karen accepted his explanation, but felt uneasy anyway. She felt such calls should be made from home.

The tension between Karen and Dan increased. At heart, Karen didn't trust Dan. And Dan resented Karen's attempts to restrict his freedom. Karen made it clear that if Dan really loved her, he would honor her feelings, not make secret phone calls, and cut back on his social life and the flirting that went with it. Dan made it equally clear that he thought Karen's jealousy was the real problem.

Then Dan's short affair happened.

As believers, Karen and Dan subscribed to the teachings of Christianity. Yet their faith, when Karen arrived to stay with us, was not helping them work out their problems. In fact, both of them used Bible passages to support their criticism of the other.

Through a series of conversations, with Karen directly and with Dan by phone, their separate perspectives on the problem, their emotional needs, and what each proposed as a solution became clear.

KAREN'S PERSPECTIVE

"If Dan really loved me," she said, "he would cut down on all his party-going and devote more of his attention to me. When we go to a church function or an office party, he should treat me with more consideration than the other women there." Karen referred to 1 Pet. 3:7: "You husbands likewise, live with your wives in an understanding way; . . . and grant her honor as a fellow heir of the grace of life." Karen remembered how Dan had longed to be with her every waking hour while they were dating. She found it impossible to understand why she couldn't fill Dan's need for friendship. She wanted to, badly.

KAREN'S NEED

Karen needed to feel loved. She often said, "All I want is for Dan to *really* love me." She wanted more of Dan's attention as proof of his love for her.

KAREN'S "SOLUTION"

Karen believed the fulfillment of her longing for love depended on her husband. She believed that if Dan would honor her according to God's Word (1 Pet. 3:7), the problem would be solved.

Karen and Dan

DAN'S PERSPECTIVE

Dan felt misunderstood and threatened. He thought it unfair to be accused of not loving his wife because he had other friends. A wife, he thought, should not be contentious and jealous; she should submit to her husband's wishes, and, in this case, she should never have complained about Dan's social life. All of her haranguing had led to the affair; she had driven him into the other woman's arms.

DAN'S NEED

Dan needed to know he was loved. He wanted to feel appreciated and respected by others, as well as by his wife.

DAN'S "SOLUTION"

Dan believed his need for love and respect would be fulfilled by both his wife and friends. Dan was convinced that if Karen would understand his need to be appreciated, respected, and looked up to, as well as his need for additional friends, the problem would be solved.

Obviously, Karen and Dan had reached a point of stalemate. They both needed to know they were loved, but with the tensions that existed between them, how could they?

3

Unlocking the Secret to Love

L et's face it. Some biblical concepts are tough to apply. For instance, Jesus said, "love one another even as I have loved you" (John 13:34). It's not easy to love as Christ loved, especially in a loveless world. Mostly, our human love is based on a condition: I'll love you if you love me. That's the only kind of love most of us know. And to be hit with the command "love one another unconditionally!" seems absurd, especially in our highly competitive society where people climb on top of and *over* their friends in a mad scramble up the ladder of success. Clearly, human strategies for implementing divine instructions on love aren't likely to work. God's plan for love in human relationships works on His principles, or not at all.

Karen, because of deep insecurity, depended completely on Dan's fulfilling her need for love, but she was continually anxious about being betrayed. The amorous attention Dan paid other women at parties caused her to put more and more pressure on Dan to love her and her only. Dan thought her demands were not only inappropriate but unbiblical. As a submissive wife, he reasoned, she should understand his desire to be liked and respected by friends. Even so, he tried to meet his wife's demands, but he only bottled up for a time the impulse that led him to seek a nonstop social life and its not-quite-innocent pleasures. In the end, he had become involved in a short affair, making up for lost time. And that's when Karen came to see us.

The devastating pain of Dan's betrayal was to be seen in the tears that welled up so quickly in Karen's eyes and the tight lips that barely restrained the scream that wanted to explode. At times like this, sometimes our silent presence can be of most help. Nice clichés and ready advice sound empty and cheap in the face of this kind of heartache. Waiting for the right moment to speak, I inwardly recoiled from the situation, particularly because the advice my wife and I were about to share would surely smart. Karen had to know that she was partly responsible for the impasse to which her marriage had come.

Then my wife and I pointed out to her, from a purely practical standpoint, that her tactics were not only proving ineffectual but were actually driving Dan further from her. Dan had to be free to respond to her willingly, for love can never be demanded but only nurtured. One must have the *free* choice to love or one does not love at all. Karen finally had to admit that the more she tried to force Dan to obey the marriage vows, the guiltier she felt and the worse the relationship became.

So what should she do? She had to begin again to love Dan, and to love him as God loves us. God's love for us in Christ models this type of no-strings-attached kind of love. "God demonstrated His own love toward us," the Apostle Paul tells us, "in that while we were yet sinners, Christ died for us" (Rom. 5:8). God doesn't demand, harangue, or threaten us if we don't respond to His overtures. He continues to draw us by the compelling force of His unquenchable love. Only as we imitate this model of love can we ever achieve God's kind of love or get the same results. It's what you might call "love, period," or, to use the Greek word, *agape.* From a psychological slant you can also call it unconditional love. This love considers the other person's needs first, even when one's own needs are greater. It complements friendship and romance with the power to give and keep on giving even when the other is unloving. It makes no demands. It is infinitely patient.

Karen's error was that she knew a lot about the teachings of Christianity, but, like most of us, not enough about the Teacher. Karen needed to "turn her eyes upon Jesus" again, and let the things of this earth, her own natural desires, grow dim until she was "alone with the Alone."

But how?

In Christian circles today there are two popular schools of thought that teach different ways of imitating Christ in giving love. They are at polar extremes. The first school is the Jesus-will-love-through-me camp. This school teaches passivity. You just wait for Jesus to pour His love through you. Stay still; wait; have faith in God, because you can't love at all. You are simply the conduit of God's love.

There's a lot of truth in this view. But it's only half the story, half the truth.

The other school emphasizes action. It is characterized by an I-will-do-it-all-by-myself theology. This school says that Jesus set the pace and gave us His example. So, you Christians, set your mind in gear (or gird up your loins) and do as Jesus did! The do-it-yourself theologians haul out their self-help kits and urge us to give our all for Jesus. They point to those troubling passages in Scripture that outline our duties and responsibilities.

Which is right?

Well, they're both right. You must *cooperate* with what God wants to do through you. You must *choose* to love, yet by faith rely on God's love to be expressed through you. God has the resource, you have the will; both must be joined together. But don't be mistaken. *You're* the one doing the loving. You don't get bypassed in some mystical switchola.

Paul strikes the balance beautifully in Phil. 4:13: "I can do all things through Him [Christ] who strengthens me." Learning to love unconditionally requires God's Spirit to do through you what you can't do. You must actively cooperate in that process, though, through acting on your faith in God.

But how, practically speaking, do you cooperate with God in order to love others with His love? When Karen was ready, I suggested three basic steps to loving and feeling God's love. They are not three steps to relational bliss. These are not easy steps. There's nothing quick and easy about loving unconditionally. It requires a new way of thinking and a new set of values founded on God's Word. But at each step along the way you will discover how faith enables you to love, what that means to you, and how that applies to your life.

The steps are:

1. Place your ultimate expectations for love in God alone.

2. Release others from binding expectations.

3. Personally accept God's provision of love through others.

Karen's main hang-up was that she didn't see how she could feel loved even when Dan wouldn't love her as he should. What she had to learn was more about the character of the God who did and always would love her.

WHERE TO PLACE
YOUR EXPECTATIONS FOR LOVE

In order to follow through on the first step in loving others as God loves you, you have to immerse yourself in the knowledge of *how* God *loves* you.

First of all, know that His love is absolutely dependable. One of the shattering disappointments Karen experienced was that the enduring love she thought she had with Dan seemed to vanish. We all want to be assured of our loved one's commitment. But there is a love you can always count on, 100 percent of the time. Without fail. If your expectations of love are centered in God, you can be confident you will be eternally loved. This assurance is founded upon God's integrity and His power (He is omnipotent) to fulfill His promises. God's love will always be there. He never runs short of love, for His love is the beginning and end of all things, just as He is. Speaking of God's love, Jeremiah writes, "I have loved you with an everlasting love. Therefore I have drawn you with lovingkindness" (31:3).

Karen had ample reason to feel pain and heartbreak because of Dan's unfaithfulness. But her unrealistic expectation that her desire for love could find its ultimate reference point in Dan compounded the problem. When Dan's love wavered, Karen was devastated. Yet, even in her pain, the objective reality was that she was still loved, and loved perfectly, by her infinite Lord.

A LOVE WITHOUT CONDITIONS

Again, there are no conditions to God's love. Karen knew that in her jealous, vindictive, and quarrelsome mental state, she wasn't as lovable as at other times. But Dottie and I were able to tell her that God's love pays no attention to our present disposition. His love says, "I love you in spite of what you may be like deep inside. I love you no matter what changes about you. You can't do a thing to turn my love off. I love you . . . period."

Paul speaks of this joyful reality in Romans 8:

> For I am convinced that nothing can ever separate us from His love. Death can't, and life can't. The angels won't, and all the powers of hell itself cannot keep God's love away. Our fears of today, our worries about tomorrow, or where we are—high above the sky, or in the deepest ocean—nothing will ever be able to separate us from the love of God demonstrated by our Lord Jesus Christ when He died for us (Rom. 8:38–39, LB).

Nevertheless, God's love is not blind. God knows everything about you and still He loves you. Your shortcomings, your faults, even your flagrant sins—God knows all these things and still loves you. "And hope does not disappoint, because the love of God has been poured out within our hearts through the Holy Spirit who was given to us. For while we were still helpless, at the right time Christ died for the ungodly" (Rom. 5:5–6).

God's love cannot be earned. His love isn't generated by some quality in the person being loved; it is generated by the character of the One who loves, God Himself. God begins loving us without our ever doing one thing to merit His favor or concern. In fact, your love for God is only possible because of God's prior love for you: "We love Him because He first loved us" (1 John 4:19, KJV). The whole life and ministry of Jesus, especially His death, as the Apostle points out, testifies to this. Jesus' mission in life was to love us first. It is His loving you first that frees you and motivates you to love Him back, and in loving Him, to allow Him to rule your life.

When you believe God's love is both eternal and unconditional, you can feel loved even when loved ones fail to love you as they should. Karen had to claim by faith God's love for her and *act upon that claim.*

HOW TO RELEASE OTHERS FROM
BINDING EXPECTATIONS

Now don't misunderstand. It's both natural and appropriate to have expectations of others. Dan had made specific commitments to Karen. Karen had pledged herself to Dan and kept that pledge. It would be logical for her to assume that Dan would keep his word. But when Dan proved unfaithful, did Karen have the right to *demand,* as she did, that Dan hold to his original marriage vows? How could faith in God equip Karen to release Dan from her "binding" expectations?

The answer is found in two simple steps.

MAKING A BIBLICAL RESPONSE TO
UNJUST TREATMENT

Expectations are essentially presumptions of how someone will act or perform in a given situation. Karen's expectations of Dan were based on her belief that Dan would love her and always be faithful to her. But then Dan betrayed her. How was Karen to respond? How do you respond when someone sins against your trust? The first step is to identify a biblical response.

A proper response to injustice is not natural, nor instinctive. So to teach Karen and the rest of us what our response in these situations should be, Christ demonstrated in His own life how we should act:

> For you have been called for this purpose, since Christ also suffered for you, leaving you an example for you to follow in His steps . . . [he] who committed no sin, nor was any deceit found in His mouth; and while being reviled, He did not revile in return; while suffering, He uttered no threats, but kept entrusting Himself to Him who judges righteously (1 Pet. 2:22–23).

Remember how we said Christ was able to respond lovingly to unjust treatment? Christ submitted to His accusers and didn't strike back in bitterness and resentment. He simply acted consistently with His nature. He gave love without demanding love in return. By an act of faith, He entrusted Himself to a Father who wouldn't let injustice go unnoticed. His Father would judge in due time.

Peter's inspired commentary lays the foundation for appropriate Christian responses in a variety of difficult relationships. He instructs all of us how we are to respond to human institutions of authority: citizens to governments, servants to their masters, wives to husbands, and husbands to wives. He relates all these situations to how Christ responded when He was accused unjustly and suffered mistreatment:

> To sum up, let all be harmonious, sympathetic, brotherly, kind-hearted, and humble in spirit; not returning evil for evil, or insult for insult, but giving a blessing instead; for you were called for the very purpose that you might inherit a blessing (1 Pet. 3:8–9).

Karen had been "reviled" by Dan. She had a natural right to protest, just as Christ did. But what did Christ do? He submitted to His accusers and suffered unjust treatment because He believed His Father would eventually judge rightly. What was Karen to do?

> In the same way [the manner of Christ], you wives, be submissive to your own husbands so that even if any of them are disobedient to the word, they may be won without a word by the behavior of their wives, as they observe your chaste and respectful behavior (1 Pet. 3:1–2).

Let's focus momentarily on that troublesome word *submissive*. Dan appealed to Karen's obligation to be submissive. So many husbands, similarly, use the word in a manipulative way. A wife's submission to her husband does *not* entail being obedient to his every whim. Peter's definition of submission is the submission Christ manifested when "they hurled their insults at him, [and] he did not retaliate; when he suffered, [and] he made no threats" (1 Pet. 2:23, NIV). *The submission of wives is the same submission with which workers, friends, and husbands are all supposed to respond to mistreatment.* This submission releases the other from *selfish, binding expectations based on "rights."* It yields to injustice and returns good for evil. It requires more of a concern for the other's needs than one's own.

The way in which you can keep from placing selfish and binding expectations on others is to believe God will judge rightly and then allow the Holy Spirit to bathe you in His love. This is where faith connects with love.

Do you believe God is fair? Do you believe He judges rightly? If you believe that, if you entrust yourself to the One who will rightly judge your offender, you are free to love your offender. Note that I didn't say you would be free to *approve* but to *love* him or her. God doesn't approve of Dan's unfaithfulness and neither should Karen. God is not going to let wrong go unpunished. You and I don't have to demand our rights. God will judge those who violate our rights—it's His responsibility to settle the score, not ours. Rest your case at the bar of His righteous justice and love those who offend you, we are told. This kind of love is not easy and does not come naturally, but you do have a will, and that will can appeal to the Spirit of God for help. Christ wants you to love as He loves and He will supply the grace for you, if only you prepare your heart to accept it.

The most effective way to receive God's grace in such times of crisis is to cry for help *within the context of praise.* By the act of your will you can identify the response you desire and praise God for being not only your righteous judge, but you can also praise Him for being your loving friend, who will love through you with His supernatural love. Praise Him for being the love you need. Praise Him for loving you unconditionally. Praise Him for His example in returning love for insults and cruelty. Praise Him for being the Incarnation of that love which would, and finally will, transform all such situations. In this way praise will activate your faith to receive God's love.

Don't underestimate the value of praise. There is something about expressing your appreciation to God in words, song, and meditation that solidifies your faith. The Book of Psalms is the Bible's hymnal of praise. The more you praise God for being who He is—a loving God who judges rightly— the more you can act upon your belief of what He is—eternal love.

PURIFYING YOUR MOTIVES

The second step in learning not to place others under burdensome expectations is to allow the Spirit of God to purify your motives. At first, Karen could not detect an improper motive on her part. Dan was the one who was unfaithful. She had a right to demand Dan to stay true to her. Dan took the marriage vows by choice, and she felt it only fair he keep them.

There's nothing wrong with those expectations—unless they are laced with selfish motivations. The issue is not really the expectations as much as the motivation that generates our expectations. *Selfish* expectations bind and stifle relationships.

At this point the let-Jesus-love-through-you camp tips its scales toward error. In their sincere attempt to present God's truth, teachers who operate within this school of thought suggest we just clam up, accept what life brings us, and never speak of our rights. That sounds oh-so-spiritual until you realize that *God* says He gives us certain rights. That's clear, biblically. *God* expected Dan to love his wife and fulfill her needs by living with her "in an understanding way . . . [granting] her honor as a fellow heir of the grace of life, so that your prayers may not be hindered" (1 Pet. 3:7). The question is, on what were God's expectations of Dan based? *Why* did God demand fidelity of Dan? God's expectations for both Dan and Karen—for all of us—were and are based on His desire to protect us and provide for us. God expected Dan to love his wife faithfully *for Dan's own good.* God knows that love is most fulfilling when exercised in the context of commitment. He wanted Dan to be happy, and Karen too. It wasn't selfish for God to have this expectation of Dan; it was loving.

Similarly, our motives for expecting others to fulfill their responsibilities should be based on what is best for them—on love. Karen had every right to expect faithfulness of Dan. But her biblical obligation as a wife to hold him to his commitments should have been based on a loving concern for him. God never releases Dan, nor does He release us, from His admonitions that we live according to principle. Neither should Karen have released Dan from his obligation to love faithfully. What Karen had to do was release Dan from *selfishly* binding expectations. God's love has no strings attached. Ours must not either. Karen had to learn how to yield her personal expectations and put her husband's welfare first. She had to realize that Dan was the one in real trouble. Dan was failing to trust God to provide sufficiently for him, giving evidence that he did not trust God to protect and provide for him. Karen had to respond to Dan on the basis of *the real problem.*

Again the issue is not our expectations, it's our *selfish* expectations. What stings our hearts, gnaws our souls, creates havoc and chaos in relationships, is the selfish motivations underlying our unfulfilled expectations. We want our loved ones to perform, shape up, or meet our needs for *our* sake, not God's. Nothing exposes our motives more quickly than for loved ones, friends, even acquaintances, not to live up to our expectations. And nothing creates bitterness, resentment, or unforgiveness more quickly than unfulfilled, selfish expectations.

God loves you, and He won't let you down. God will judge your offenders. He will demand their obedience; you don't need to place binding expectations upon them. Let your expectations go; release others from them. Keep faith in a just God who loves you, and you will take a major step toward purifying your motives and releasing others from selfish expectations.

The hurt from Dan's unfaithfulness was replaced by genuine concern as Karen saw the consequences of Dan's sin unfold in his life. When she released him from her selfish expectations she was truly free for the first time to challenge him to live up to his biblical responsibilities as a husband. It was the loving thing to do then, for only in fidelity would Dan ever experience the wealth of love given in a solid marriage.

WHY GOD'S CHOICES CAN IMPROVE
YOUR RELATIONSHIPS

Right now you may need to know you are loved for who you are, and it is painful not to sense that. God has made you with that need and most often chooses to provide for you through others. Accepting God's choices often improves your relationships because you view them as an integral part of God's plan for you. Placing your expectations for love in God alone and releasing any selfish demands on others prepares you to be content with the channels through whom God chooses to communicate His love. This also is a step of faith.

BEING CONTENT WITH GOD'S TIMING

God plans to meet your needs. Only, He will do so on His timetable. Often your faith is tested in whether you are willing to rest in the knowledge that God's timing is best. You may believe that God will finally institute universal justice, but you may still become anxious and dispute why He chooses to withhold His judgment of the evildoer and His mercy to the righteous. But you are not to take matters into your own hands. God has promised to provide for you in "due time" (Ps. 145:15). Some versions overlay the phrase *due time* with the implication of "ripeness," a time that is appropriate and as if succulent by virtue of its growth or preparation.

God has a design and plan to provide for you, and waiting to follow His prescribed timetable will be in your best interest. It is rewarding to share with young people, for example, how God's principles for love, sex, and marriage imposes a sequence, which results in a timetable that—no matter how difficult to bear—is a light yoke in comparison to the effects of promiscuity. It always pays to wait, especially when God is keeping time.

BEING CONTENT WITH GOD'S CHOICES

Being satisfied with God's provisions includes being satisfied with the channels God uses. Yet, sometimes those through whom God chooses to provide love need to change in various ways for their own good, and ours. How can this dilemma be resolved? Karen struggled in this area. She realized that if God was to provide through Dan, he would need to change drastically in his actions and especially his attitudes.

Yet Karen's attempts to change Dan by making demands were not successful. Coercion creates resistance to change, as you will remember. This is precisely where we must apply our understanding that God as the ultimate source of love perfectly loves us even though that love may be imperfectly expressed by those close to us.

I've had some say to me, "If I place my expectations in God and release binding expectations in my companion, he (or she) will never change for the better." That may be the surface appearance, but the very opposite is true. A lot of men will say, "Hey, if I loved my girl in spite of the way she looks or does things, she'd never change for the better." Yes, she would. Because unconditional love is a giving love. It is actually God's love poured through an individual, and it's so winsome, so irresistible that it draws out the best in the other person. It causes creative changes in the other person. The changes aren't demanded; they are simply a natural response to unconditional love.

In reality, you see, you cannot force another person to change. Only that person can change himself. But through Christ *you* can change *yourself.* When *you* change, when you begin to act differently to someone else, *that person begins to change.* It sounds incredible, yet it works time after time.

That is exactly what happened in Karen and Dan's case. For the first time, Karen began to release Dan from her demands. As she placed her ultimate trust in a loving God whom she believed in as her provider and protector, she was given the grace to love Dan unconditionally. Her love no longer depended on Dan's response. This motivated Dan to repent and change. This joyful solution does not always come about. Though God draws all men and women to repentance with His love, not all repent. But Karen was a beautiful, real-life example of a wife yielding her rights to God "so that even if any of them [husbands] are disobedient to the word, they may be won without a word by the behavior of their wives, as they observe your chaste and respectful behavior" (1 Pet. 3:1–2).

All God's choices test our faith that God knows best. It tests our commitment to God as our loving provider. What if God chooses to postpone a provision for what seems to you an unreasonable period of time? How about God withholding indefinitely a provision that seems essential? Perhaps God has chosen a means of provision that you don't find readily acceptable. What then?

You have a choice to make. Either you chafe under the apparent injustice or rest by faith in the One who does all things well. Do you believe God is your loving provider and protector? Do you believe God loves you eternally and unconditionally? Do you believe He will rightly judge all those who violate your rights? If so, let your faith release others from selfish demands and allow God to show His love through you. Direct action in this regard will help you *experience* through faith the love of God.

As stressed earlier, the deeper your acquaintance with Christ, the more you are convinced He has your best interest at heart. God's moral boundaries are not given because God wishes to withhold any good thing from you, but to maximize your happiness. Your joy of loving and being loved is in Christ. All your expectations for love should be centered in Him. In God's time the longings of your heart will be fulfilled. Remember King David. Remember Dan. Remember how Karen found the essential connection between faith and love.

If you have not made this connection, examine God's Word deeply. Seek to know Him for who and what He is, and you will see that He is completely worthy of your trust. Paul said, "He who did not spare His own Son, but delivered Him up for us all, how will He not also with Him freely give us all things?" (Rom. 8:32).

4

Love and Limits

C S. Lewis reports that a schoolboy was once asked what he thought God was like. He replied, "The sort of person who is always snooping around to see if anyone is enjoying himself and then trying to stop it."

I'm afraid that's the sort of idea in many Christians' minds whenever God's law is discussed: God's law interferes with your freedom and keeps you from having a good time. But "God is love" and thus God's law, as an expression of His character, is also an expression of love. The realization that God has our good in mind in setting down limitations will give us a whole new perspective for getting to know the kind of God we serve. God doesn't issues commands to cramp our lifestyle and limit our liberty. Instead, His law defines the limits in which our liberty can be fully expressed.

The Old Testament writers understood God's motivation in setting down His law. Deuteronomy emphasizes this:

> And now, Israel, what does the Lord your God require from you, but to fear the Lord your God, to walk in all His ways and love Him, and to serve the Lord your God with all your heart and with all your soul, and to keep the Lord's commandments and His statutes *which I am commanding you today for your good?* (10:12–13, my emphasis).

Moses articulates here God's motivation for giving Israel the law: *for your good.* This same point is scattered throughout Deuteronomy (cf. 5:29; 6:18; 8:18; 30:15–20).

I live in southern California, and to drive on the freeways there is the experience of a lifetime. Even with the traffic laws, there are times you have to literally drive for your life! The laws define the way the traffic moves: when you must stop, how you may turn, how fast you may travel. All those regulations are for the good of the motorist, to ensure his safety and provide good driving conditions. I don't chafe under the law that says you must drive on the right-hand side of the road. That regulation defines a pattern for safe driving.

We need to understand God's law in the same way. Acknowledge that God knows best and that He knows just what you need for happy, fulfilled living. So obey His commands, not out of the fear of getting zapped if you don't, but in the knowledge that His law expresses God's best for you. We are created by divine design to function best within the context of God's laws. If we disregard God's laws in sin, we crash—and suffer the consequences.

In fact when God issues a negative command there are always two positive motives behind it: one to protect you and the other to provide for you.

The Danger from Ourselves

God desires to protect us from the harm of our ill-informed choices. He gives us His law so that we won't try to meet our own needs and miserably fail—and suffer the consequences! He loves us so much that He wants to protect us from the pain that will surely result from pursuing our own choices. His law maps out His step-by-step plan for doing just that.

Sin always brings destruction: spiritually, mentally, and physically. He gives His law, then, to guide us away from those choices that would bring us pain. As a child of God I want to live compatibly with His nature, and His law gives me those guidelines. The law identifies many wrong choices that might otherwise look harmless.

Finding Real Happiness

Also, if God is love (and He is), and if you're His dear child, then the law defines how a loving God has chosen to provide for you. When God says, "Don't," you know He has other, even better, provisions to give you if you will obey Him.

It's in this context that the Psalm writer claims, "No good thing does He withhold from those who walk uprightly" (Ps. 84:11). Also, "They who seek the Lord shall not be in want of any good thing" (Ps. 34:10). God wants to meet your needs. He's able to do anything. Yet, if He's withholding something from you, by virtue of issuing a command against it, you can rest assured it's because He has something better in store for you later.

I understood this when I broke up with a girl I was engaged to. I loved her and thought she was everything I ever wanted in a wife. Yet God wouldn't give us peace about our relationship. And it hurt to break off that relationship. I remember when my plane rolled away from the gate where I had left her, having seen her for possibly the last time, I thought my heart would break. I was angry at God. I wanted to run off that plane and shout, "I love you! Let's get married."

Yet I knew that was wrong. As the plane taxied to the runway, I prayed, angrily. "God, how can you be so unloving, so uncaring?"

"Josh," God seemed to say, "I will withhold no good thing. . . ."

"Is this a 'good thing'? It hurts!"

"I will withhold no good thing. . . ."

"But what about *her*? She's the best thing that ever happened to me!"

And then it seemed I understood, "Then . . . the woman you will give me will be better than her?" No, that didn't seem right.

"Not necessarily better than Paula," God seemed to say, "but better for *you* than Paula. I'm not punishing you. I only want the best for you."

Because I serve a God who loves me and provides for me, and has proven that in the past, in my life and in the lives of others, I was able to accept momentary heartache in

47

anticipation of the greater good God was bringing to me. The struggle was made easier because I knew why He directed me to give up Paula: it was not only for my present good as well as future happiness, but also for His glory. However, it still hurt.

God is such a loving provider. Trusting Him to know what is best and following His guidelines will maximize your happiness and meet your need for love every time. It wasn't until several years later that I truly understood this principle. Breaking off my relationship with Paula greatly tested my faith at the time to believe that God knew what He was doing and was reserving His best for me. But when I met and married Dottie, I learned that God *had* reserved the best for last. I wouldn't trade my relationship with my wife for anything. She's just what I need—God's perfect provision for me.

I call Psalms the praise book on God's abilities and character. In Psalm 145 David clearly declares God's motivation to provide for you and protect you. Read it and see how it expresses God's loving intent. I'm selecting key verses to show you what I mean.

Protection (v. 14): "The Lord sustains all who fall, And raises up all who are bowed down."

Provision (vv. 15–16): "The eyes of all look to Thee, And Thou dost give them their food in due time. Thou dost open Thy hand, And dost satisfy the desire of every living thing."

Protection (v. 18): "The Lord is near to all who call upon Him, To all who call upon Him in truth."

Provision (vv. 19–20): "He will also hear their cry and will save them. The Lord keeps all who love Him; But all the wicked, He will destroy."

GOD'S PROTECTION AND PROVISION:
CHOOSING OR REJECTING

Isn't it exciting to realize that God's motivation, in prohibiting certain things for you, is to protect you from destructive influences that you could never foresee? In essence, God is saying, "Josh, Dale, Karen, Dan, [your name] wait! Because I love you so much, I'm going to protect you from anything that would keep you from living an abundant life." When you understand this concept, your outlook on God's law changes. You can see a God of love who uses His law as guidelines enabling you to achieve fulfillment and joy in life. No longer do you have to chafe under what you think are restrictions that inhibit your liberty. His guidelines for life are designed to maximize your happiness.

On the other hand, when you fail to trust God as your ultimate provider and protector, eventually you will almost certainly attempt to illegitimately meet your own needs. You always have two choices: (1) trust God that He is able and willing to meet your needs; or (2) selfishly attempt to fulfill your own needs.

Choosing between the two seems easy at first. You and I, as armchair theorists, would quickly agree that trusting Christ is the best course of action. But Satan is deceitful. One of his favorite strategies is to disguise wrong choices as good ones. He obviously doesn't want you to see how sin will bring grief and sorrow into your life. No one in his right mind would purposely choose grief and suffering. So Satan distracts our attention from the evil consequences of sin, and he represents the sinful choice as appealing, irresistible, and even necessary.

King David is a classic example of one who sought to meet his own needs apart from God. You no doubt know the story of David and Bathsheba; it's one of the greatest dramas of the Bible. Under the reign of King David, the tiny nation of Israel had grown to a place of respect and prestige among her neighboring kingdoms. At the tail end of a war, while the army was sweeping the hillsides on search-and-destroy missions, David was at home with time on his hands. While strolling on his palace rooftop one day he saw a beautiful woman bathing next door. Lust made his heart race. He inquired about her. Her name was Bathsheba, and she was the wife of one of his soldiers, Uriah.

The story is told in undisguised detail in 2 Samuel 11. David took Bathsheba into his palace and slept with her. She became pregnant. Faced with this embarrassing situation, David tried to cover his sin. He brought Uriah home from the front lines to make it appear that Uriah was the father of the unborn child. But Uriah felt it would be wrong of him to enjoy his home and family while his fellows were camping in the open field. In devotion to his king and the cause of Israel, he slept on the palace steps. What would David do now? The king finally ordered Uriah back to the front lines, giving instructions by letter to his field general, Joab, that Uriah was to fight on the front lines, and then, with the rest of the army falling back, be abandoned to fight and die alone. The orders given to Uriah amounted to a death warrant. The execution came off as scheduled. David was then free to take Bathsheba as his wife.

Months went by. Bathsheba moved into the palace, and it looked like David was home free. Yet God wouldn't let David off the hook. God marshaled one of his prophets, Nathan, and told him to go to the palace and tell David a story about a rich man, a poor man, and a lone sheep.

Nathan told David that the rich man had great flocks of sheep, but the poor man had only one ewe which he had reared as if it had been his child, feeding it from his own cup at the table. A visitor came to the city, and instead of the rich man slaughtering one of his own sheep, he took the poor man's sheep and served it to his guest. David became angry, and burst out, "As the Lord lives, the man who did this deserves to die!" Nathan pointed his bony finger under David's nose and bellowed, "You are the man" (2 Sam. 2:16–17).

What was David's primary sin? Was it lust, adultery, deception, murder? David had surely committed all these sins. Yet, when convicted by Nathan's words David cried, "I have sinned against the Lord" (2 Sam. 12:13). A strange thing to say, isn't it, after someone has committed adultery and murder? Yet David's penitential prayer in Psalm 51 echoes this same theme: "Against Thee, Thee only, I have sinned, and done what is evil in Thy sight, so that Thou art justified when Thou dost speak, and blameless when Thou dost judge" (v. 4).

David did sin against Bathsheba, Uriah, and others. But that was not his primary sin. His first sin was against God, distrusting Him as his loving provider and protector. The other sins were the consequences of his offense against God. Note Nathan's declaration of what God wanted to say to David:

> "Thus says the Lord God of Israel, 'It is I who anointed you king over Israel, and it is I who delivered you from the hand of Saul. I also gave you your master's house and your master's wives into your care, and I gave you the house of Israel and Judah; and if that had been too little, I would have added to you many more things like these!'" (2 Sam. 12:7–8).

God had given David everything he needed and more, and if David had needed something more, God would have even given him that. But what did David do? He quit trusting God as his provider. The Scripture clearly isolates David's sin against God. "Why have you despised the Word of the Lord by doing evil in His sight?" (2 Sam. 12:9). David despised, "counted worthless," God's provisions.

Mark it down and remember it. Whenever Satan tempts you to cross the line of God's moral boundaries with the promise to fulfill a need you feel you have, it's a lie. Any provision Satan provides is an illusion, a mirage of the reality there is in Christ. Only Christ is able truly to meet your needs.

In David's life God has given us a picture of both His mercy and the destructive consequences of sin. Even though David was restored to fellowship with God, he had to suffer the consequences of his sin. The baby that was the result of David and Bathsheba's union died; one of David's daughters, Tamar, was raped by her brother; Absalom fomented a rebellion and was killed by David's own men. Indeed, for the rest of his reign, David was haunted by bloodshed, turmoil, and conspiracy.

"Without faith it is impossible to please Him," the writer of Hebrews says (11:6). "Whatever is not from faith is sin," explains the Apostle Paul (Rom. 14:23). The root cause of sin is disbelief. And the cause of King David's tragedy was a failure to rest in, depend upon, and trust in the one Person that has promised to "satisfy the desires of every living thing."

Later, years after his taking of Bathsheba, David learned that faith in God's timing was essential to a restored, happy life, and he accepted God's timetable. The songs of David record praises to God as a faithful provider for this reason. David's experience in learning to trust God as provider and protector gives the words of Psalm 37 special significance: "Delight yourself in the Lord; And He will give you the desires of your heart. Commit your way to the Lord, Trust also in Him, and He will do it" (vv. 4–5).

This is David's answer to a joyful life of loving and being loved. *Delight, trust,* and *commit* your way to the Lord. A trust relationship with a loving God empowers you to live according to His principles of life. No, joy is not in just following rules; it is in trusting a loving God who is both willing and able to provide your needs and protect you from harm.

I didn't get married until I was thirty-two. I've always said that if you want a queen for a wife, be a king! And over the years God faithfully gave me the opportunity to apply that challenge and develop into the kind of person I needed to be as a husband. And the process isn't over yet!

As you can imagine, I dated several Christian women. I thank God for those friendships because through them I was brought closer to Christ. Yet, in dating, I had to discipline my thought-life and behavior in order to conform to God's standards for singles. As I grew older, I wondered if God really had a woman especially for me and whether God's principles for love and sex were really to be exercised only in the context of a marriage commitment. I'm glad now I held steady. My heart aches to see unmarried men and women engaging in behavior that I know will rob them of the maximum relationship that God intends for them in the area of love, sex, and marriage. What made it easier to wait was the realization, embedded deep in my mind, that I served a God who had my best interests at heart and who would withhold from me only those things that would be harmful and destructive. I realized that, by telling me to wait, God was both providing for my best interest and protecting me from the devastation, heartache, and emptiness caused by sin.

Dottie loves to tell how she and I met six or seven times and I never remembered her. She says that was humbling. I can understand why, but we're both convinced now this happened because even though we were always the right ones for each other, in God's eyes neither one of us was ready for a permanent relationship. The first time we met I had just returned from many months in Latin America and had just begun my traveling ministry in the United States. Dottie, who is seven and a half years younger than I, was just beginning to work with the Campus Crusade for Christ movement at the University of Texas. God knew we both needed more time as singles so He allowed us to meet on six more occasions before I even recognized her. Then in a crowd of over a thousand at an outdoor free speech rally, I spotted Dottie sitting on the grass in the back of a crowd, and I never forgot again. That was

God's perfect timing. I believe He removed my blinders so I could clearly see the gift He had ready for me.

God's law flows from His motivation to provide for you and protect you. You may not always know why you suffer momentary deprivation in this life as a result of a restriction or limitation He has imposed. But you can always rest assured it is because God loves you. Place your faith *in Him*. What He withholds He withholds for your good.

5

A Case for Rejection

If there is any problem that closely follows people's fear of not being able to give or receive love, it is the problem of low self-esteem. Sad to say, most people simply do not like themselves. Tall people wish they were shorter; short people wish they were taller. Thin people wish they were heavier; heavy people wish they were thinner. We all wish to be different in some way.

My own self-image began changing from negative to positive once I started building a healthy sense of acceptance. But that change was not the result of some pop psychological pep talk I gave myself—a "you're a winner, you're a winner" piece of jargon said ten times each morning in the mirror. No, it was a process much more profound and much more lasting. I discovered that my acceptance was grounded in *God's* nature—who He was and who I was in Him. The knowledge of *that* truth is what really changed my inner sense of worth and value. I found a direct relationship between my *faith* in God and my acceptance of myself. When I *believed* I was truly accepted, my self-concept was affected.

While I was a student at Kellogg College, you will recall, my self-esteem was at its all-time low. At that point I thought faith was subjective, that how much faith a person had was more important than what or why one believed. But working harder to believe only led to continued failure and a lack of confidence in myself.

In continuing "my search," I discovered (much to my relief) that faith was not subjective, but objective. True Christian faith focuses on Jesus Christ as its object and what *He* thinks of me as a person. When you know why you believe in Him, you are "persuaded that *He* is able to keep that which [you] have committed unto Him."

Mike and Sue are friends who, possibly like you, struggled with their need for acceptance. They too believed faith was subjective, and they held this view long after becoming Christians. Mike and Sue had a good marriage, an active church life, and two precocious teenage children. Mike had started his own advertising business, and the business had been growing steadily. Mike was well educated, sophisticated, and articulate. Sue married Mike before she finished her last year of college. Mike assured her she could finish and get her degree sometime after they married, but she never pursued it further. Mike was from the Deep South, and Sue from a New England state. They were now living in the South. Mike and Sue's social life revolved around Mike's business contacts and associates. Mike and Sue appeared to be a model couple.

But Sue was struggling deep inside with feelings of rejection that brought on periodic bouts of depression. These were usually triggered by incidents involving Mike's friends and associates, who would occasionally joke about her New England accent, or insinuate that she was not as educated as her husband. Sue so badly wanted these people to accept her, yet nothing seemed to work. In tears and frustration she asked, "Why can't people accept me for who I am? I feel like Mike's friends want me to be somebody I'm not. I just can't fit into their mold. Why can't just being me be enough?"

Charles Cooley, regarded by many as one of the most brilliant American sociologists, propagated a concept called the "looking-glass self." This view essentially states that a person's self-concept is largely determined by what he/she believes the most important person in his/her life thinks about him/her.

Sue was an extreme case in point. Being a relational person, she found people—even casual acquaintances—very important in her life. What she believed Mike's friends thought about her affected her sense of acceptance. As Cooley points out, the battle for self-acceptance is won or lost in your mind. If you feed it false or misleading information, you set yourself up for feelings of rejection, as Sue did.

Mike was a distinctly different personality. Hard-working, goal-oriented, he loved a challenge and placed a high standard on his own performance. But Mike, like Sue, also struggled with acceptance.

For the past year Mike's advertising campaigns had not been effective for two major clients. Mike worked hard on their accounts, but no matter what he did, they failed. After losing his first client, he lamented: "I've done everything I know to do, and it's not enough. If I lose one more account, I'm ruined." The financial pressure was great, but more than that, I sensed Mike was having an identity crisis. "I may not be a failure, but at this point I sure feel like one. I have so much riding on these two accounts. I've lost one, and it doesn't look good on the other. I feel like I'm losing control. All my efforts don't seem to be enough. What am I supposed to do, Josh?"

Mike, as a goal-oriented person, had a drive to produce, achieve, and perform. It was natural for him to have a sense of inner satisfaction and gratification in knowing he had met his objectives. However, Mike allowed his faltering performance to determine his view of himself. What he believed about his ability to conduct a successful business directly affected his feelings of acceptance.

When both Mike and Sue began to examine just what they believed about themselves and why they believed it, it became clear that they based their sense of acceptance upon subjective feelings. While both had different symptoms, they both sought acceptance based on performance.

SUE'S PERSPECTIVE

Sue felt Mike's friends were unfair to look down on her. She often prayed, asking God's help to overcome her depression.

She thought if she would believe God sincerely enough, He would answer her prayer, take away her depression, and help her be a better person.

SUE'S NEED

Sue needed to know and sense she was worthwhile even though she did not measure up to other people's social standards. She needed to feel accepted for the person she was, not what others thought she should be.

SUE'S "SOLUTION"

Sue believed her acceptance came largely from people. Sue often said, "I think the problem is with people. If they were more loving and would accept me as I am, I could be my own person without feeling pressured to conform. If they only would accept me for who I am, I wouldn't be so depressed."

Simultaneously, Sue worked hard to improve her personality. She wanted to be more loving and less sensitive to people's remarks. Sue reasoned that if she could be more composed during times of crisis—like the financial crunch resulting from Mike's failing business—then others would find her more enjoyable company and would accept her.

MIKE'S PERSPECTIVE

In the wake of unsuccessful advertising campaigns, the two companies canceled their accounts. Mike said, "I've developed such rapport with those men. Why didn't they call me or come by to talk it over instead of sending letters of cancellation?" The letters were terse, cold, and unfriendly. Mike convinced himself that his "friends" were only friends because of what he could do for them. Mike felt that "if you don't put out you just won't have friends."

MIKE'S NEED

Mike needed to know he was accepted even when his performance was poor. He needed to feel worthy even when he did not meet his own standards. He needed others to accept him as he was, rather than base their friendship on what he could accomplish for them.

MIKE'S "SOLUTION"

Mike believed his acceptance largely came from what he could do. He would say, "If people would just give me the chance to accomplish my goals, rather than pull out when the going gets rough, I could produce wonders." He believed he could make each project succeed if only he were given another chance. Mike sought for God to prop up his own strength so he could do a better job next time. If only he trusted, he thought, God would enable him to be a greater success.

Would it have been possible for Mike to be rejected, even because of his performance, and still feel accepted? Could Sue have been rejected, even because of personal blind spots, and still feel accepted? Let's discover how.

6

Unlocking the Secret
to Acceptance

Mike and Sue were faced with the challenge of overcoming the mental habits and emotional responses that had long ruled their ability to deal with the rejections and failures of life. The failure of Mike's business and the ensuing financial crunch brought both Mike and Sue to a test of faith. They were forced to examine what they believed about God and why. So, it simply wasn't realistic for me to sit back in my soft office chair and tell Mike and Sue, "You're acceptable now that you're Christians; go out and feel accepted." They had to ask the questions: "Where does my faith lie? In my ability to perform up to standard? Or in Christ? Do I believe what others think about me? Or do I believe what God thinks?" In answering those questions they began to see that although their ability to perform was inadequate, Christ would not fail to perform perfectly.

Mike could no longer remain in business for himself and had to seek a position with another advertising agency. Although it was difficult for him to accept his failure, he finally came to admit to himself and to God that he could not gain acceptance by his performance. At last he was able to release his grasp on self-effort and turn to examine just what he believed about himself and why he believed it. He began to see himself in a whole new light, as accepted by God because of what Christ had done, not because of what he could do.

The change of jobs for Mike was a personal crisis for Sue as well. She began to see that she had based her self-image on the opinions of people who were part of the changing circumstances of life. Mike now had new business associates, and she would have new people whose approval she'd have to gain. She saw that it was futile to depend upon others for acceptance. The eternal, constant, and unconditional love of God was hers through Christ. Her acceptance had been won, and she received and acknowledged that acceptance.

Through the testing of their faith, Mike and Sue were able to correct their misconceptions, be strengthened in their faith, and accept with joy their new perspective of themselves and their relationship with Christ.

To accept your acceptance in Christ, to the point that you can feel accepted even when rejected by others, comes through a maturing process over a period of time. You must inform your mind and emotions with what is true of you according to God's Word. This surely is Paul's meaning when he instructs us to "be transformed by the renewing of your mind" (Rom. 12:2). You must look at life from God's perspective and not man's. Your response must be to accept, affirm, and act upon God's facts that are true of you. You *can* accept your acceptance.

ACCEPTING GOD'S VIEW AS TRUE

But that set of objective facts, as true as they may be, does not go unchallenged. At every step of your journey in this life there are at least two voices that cry out against the truth of God's Word and attempt to undermine God's authority: Satan and your past conditioning.

SATAN REMINDS US OF THE OLD FACTS

Never forget that Satan marshals his forces against you to get you to doubt God's words. He repeats his original strategy with Adam and Eve. Remember the serpent's hissing words to Eve, "Ye shall not surely die"? Let these diabolical words emblazon themselves boldly on the walls of your mind. Let yourself feel a cold shudder as you contemplate the horrifying consequences of Adam's first sin. Doubting God is precisely where sin begins.

Every day of your life you are faced with a question: do you really believe in God's Word? There are no theological abstractions to hide behind. There is no psychological profile to analyze. You are either trusting God or you are not. If you are, your life will show it. Your mind will understand the meaning of trusting God. Your emotions will feel love, acceptance, and security from that trusting relationship with God.

But how do you deal with emotions that have been scarred by past sin and childhood conditioning? Your acceptance in Christ does not automatically erase the memory of your past. Be assured the enemy makes every effort to see that you do not forget.

Prior to trusting Christ you were *not* acceptable to God. As nice as you may have appeared—you were sinful. The degree to which you *felt* unacceptable depended largely upon your past actions and childhood conditioning. If you're like most of us, you are aware that Satan has plenty of past facts of which to remind you. Those facts no doubt have been firmly established in your mind and emotions.

Now, what happens to those past facts when you trust Christ and God accepts you? Are they erased from your mind? Do your emotions, scarred by past sin, forget that negative conditioning? Unfortunately, no. Acceptance in Christ does not automatically eradicate the memory of the past.

WE REMIND OURSELVES OF THE OLD FACTS

It is quite evident in my life that I have not arrived at perfection. My old habit patterns plague me, and many areas need change in my life. I am the first to admit it. Often, as with Peter when he was walking on the water, my attention becomes distracted from looking to Christ, and I begin to look to myself. My imperfection is an ever-present voice reminding me of what yet needs to change. But I can say, that "though I am not what I ought to be, thank God I am not what I used to be; and by the grace of God I am not all I am going to be!"

While our spirits are reborn, we still have our old personalities. God intends to change our old patterns of thinking and feeling through a process of being conformed to the image of Christ. "For whom He foreknew, He also predestined to become conformed to the image of His Son, that He might be the first-born among many brethren" (Rom. 8:29). Our growth in Christ requires a process of bringing our minds and emotions into harmony with our new identity.

It may be difficult for you to grasp and accept the idea that God is *pleased* to use a process requiring time. Valuable lessons in Christlikeness are often learned through the process itself. Yet imperfect emotions, the product of sinful conditioning, argue with a powerful voice against the fact of your being accepted. Not understanding that God plans to use life's irritations to develop you into Christlikeness, you may allow your imperfections to convince you you're not acceptable. Don't do it! Accept the fact that your need for growth does not affect your acceptance. Growth, being made like Christ, is part of God's plan. Accept that plan.

Recently I struggled with my own acceptance because I was unwilling to forgive myself. During a conversation at a restaurant with some friends and associates, I said something that wounded a Christian brother who was sitting across from me. As I left the restaurant I was struck by how my remark must have sounded. I turned around, went back to the brother still sitting at the restaurant table, and sought his forgiveness. I said, "Jim, what I said a few minutes ago was wrong. I had no business saying it, and I had the wrong attitude. I've asked God to forgive me, but I sense I wounded you with my words. Will you please forgive me?"

Jim looked me straight in the eye and said, "I won't forgive you. Someone in your position should never have said what you said." I was taken aback. I have never had anyone say they would not forgive me. I thought he had misunderstood me, and I apologized again. Again Jim refused to forgive me. I left the restaurant burdened with guilt and unreconciled to my brother.

Days went by, and the incident kept coming to my mind. I would not let myself forget it. "How stupid can you be, McDowell? You know better than to say what you did. What kind of example are you for Christ? It just shows how unspiritual and immature you are. God can't use you. Your ministry is a sham. You're not what you ought to be."

But in the midst of my self-accusations and chastising, a still small voice reminded me that I was a redeemed child of God. I recalled, "There is therefore now no condemnation for those who are in Christ Jesus" (Rom. 8:1). I had not only sought God's forgiveness and received it but had also gone to my brother and sought his forgiveness.

I had a conscious choice to make: (1) look at my past sin and continue to upbraid myself about the stupidity of my wrong or (2) look to Christ's righteousness and believe that God forgives and accepts me, even if my brother does not. The choice was mine. I acknowledged God's forgiveness, forgave myself and my brother who would not forgive me, and turned the entire ordeal over to God, asking for wisdom to minister to the need of my wounded brother.

I took all the steps I could to repair the relationship with my Christian brother by seeking his forgiveness. Though it was a year before Jim's wounded spirit was healed and our relationship restored, I felt as forgiven and accepted around Jim as if he had forgiven me. Why? Because I trusted in Christ's righteousness and accepted my forgiveness in Him.

Oh, I need to grow. I know that. You see, I'm not suggesting for a moment that we should be content with unchristlike behavior. I'm suggesting that you should be content that God is maturing you into a full-grown adult, in the likeness of Christ. Because you fail does not mean you're not accepted. It means your wrong response or action was just out of character with what God wants to develop in you. Growth comes when you recognize that and work to change.

If you have trusted Christ as Savior, God is at work conforming you to Christ's image. Accept God's view of you as a cleansed, forgiven, righteous child of God, and remind yourself of it daily. Many voices will tell you otherwise, and until you rest in Christ's acceptance, you will neither feel nor act like the new creature you are becoming in Christ.

AFFIRMING YOUR POSITION IN CHRIST

If then you have been raised up with Christ, keep seeking the things above, where Christ is, seated at the right hand of God. Set your mind on the things above [objectively], not on the things that are on earth [subjectively]. For you have died and your life is hidden with Christ in God (Col. 3:1–3).

The conditional phrase beginning with *if* is a "first-class condition" in this passage. It does not mean "if, and it might be true," or "if, and it's not true," but "if, and it is true." The first-class condition is there to lend emphasis. In other words, "*since* it is true that we are seated with Christ in the heavenlies, keep seeking the things above." You do this when moment by moment you remind yourself that you are indeed positioned with Christ in the heavenlies. "Seeking" means to seek continuously in order to make application to your situation. When you "seek" for an aspirin in the medicine cabinet, you look for it in order to apply it to your headache. In the same way you are to seek the things above in order to apply them to your situation below. Do not be intent on the things on the earth (your circumstances) but be intent on the things above (your acceptance in Christ).

My personality is such that, when circumstances are against me, if I look at the situation, I'll give in, be timid, and withdraw. But daily I've learned to affirm my position in Christ. I am raised—you are raised—with Christ at the right hand of God.

That means you're accepted. Remind yourself of that every day—remind Satan of that every day. Don't let him forget it. When you're rejected by a friend or enemy, for whatever reason, affirm your position in Christ. Don't allow Satan to focus your mind subjectively on the old set of facts from the old sin life. Respond with the objective truth of God's Word. Memorize Eph. 2:4–6. Make the words personal and plant them deep within your heart. "But God, being rich in mercy, because of His great love with which He loved me, even when I was dead in my transgressions, made me alive together with Christ (by grace I have been saved), and raised me up with Him, and seated me with Him in the heavenly places, in Christ Jesus."

ACTING OUT YOUR NEW IDENTITY

What I am going to say in the last part of this section is extremely important. Read it carefully. Reread it if necessary until the truth is absorbed. I begin by stating a simple truth, not original with me, and where I got it I don't recall: "It is easier to act ourselves into a new way of feeling, than to feel ourselves into a new way of acting." On the surface that might appear to be purely a believe-yourself-into-a-winner-by-acting-like-a-winner kind of pop psychology cliché. But a closer look at Scripture reveals it to be the principle behind God's call to every Christian for obedience. Obedience to God is nothing more than acting through the Holy Spirit like the redeemed child of God you are and living out your true identity in Christ. Obedience helps you reinforce right patterns of behavior in your life, based on God's facts about you.

THE CALL TO OBEDIENCE

Therefore, gird your minds for action, keep sober in spirit, fix your hope completely on the grace to be brought to you at the revelation of Jesus Christ. As obedient children, do not be conformed to the former

71

lusts, which were yours in your ignorance (1 Pet. 1:13–14).

What is this passage challenging you to do? You are to get your mind ready for action. Fix your hope . . . where? Subjectively, on the old set of facts of your former living without Christ? No! On God's new set of facts about you, on the grace of God. You are to be an obedient child, not conformed to the old life but conformed to the new life in Christ.

Obedience does not produce a believer; but true belief will always produce obedience. And one's obedience will be consistent with one's belief. As a true believer, when you live like God's righteous child, your wounded emotions are powerfully convinced that you are acceptable.

One skillful counselor, Bob George, makes this point forcefully, showing how wrong thinking and acting influences our emotions. Bob is quoted extensively because of the need for a clear example of how acting and feeling affects our feelings of rejection:

> Now, emotions always follow thought. When someone is depressed, we say he has an emotional problem. But emotional problems, except in severe cases of physical abnormality, are caused by improper thinking.
>
> Emotions are only responders and have no intellect or intelligence of their own. They cannot distinguish between fantasy and reality or past, present or future. They merely respond predictably to whatever we are putting in our minds.
>
> People watching a horror movie experience fear even knowing there is no real monster in their room. If they know there is no reality to what they're experiencing, why do they feel fear? Because they are thinking frightening thoughts.
>
> Whatever we put in our minds determines our emotions. If we think of a sad situation, we'll feel sad. If we think of an angering situation, we'll feel anger. These things are true regardless of the reality of the thought.

The same principles hold true regarding the past or future. Our minds can instantly recall a past situation—for example, an insult. Pondering that will produce an emotion of anger just as real as when the insult first occurred.

Once we are in the grip of an emotion, such as anger, we often begin fantasizing and projecting into the future as well.

Our thought processes go something like this: "That bum insulted me" (anger). "Come to think of it, he insulted me last week too" (past thinking, more anger). "As a matter of fact, he's always treated me that way!" (beginning to fantasize, more anger).

"Everybody treats me like dirt" (fantasizing, anger, self-pity). "People will always treat me like nothing" (jump to future, fantasizing, self-pity, anger).

Sustained thinking like this will produce depression.

THE SECRET TO OBEDIENCE

The Apostle Paul gives you the secret to obedience in Rom. 6:16–19. "Do you not know that when you present yourselves to someone as slaves for obedience, you are slaves of the one whom you obey, either of sin resulting in death, or of obedience resulting in righteousness [acceptance]?" (v. 16). Imagine a sixteenth-century scene. You are standing before two powerful monarchs and are free to choose to which leader you will give allegiance. You walk up to the one of your choice, drop to your knees, and proclaim, "Your wish is my command." Your new commander knights you into his army, and you are sworn to protect and fight for his crown. You willingly choose to serve this king as a loyal subject. That is the imagery Paul projects in Romans by such words as *reign* (6:13), which comes from the root word for king; and *slave* (6:16), subjecting ourselves willingly to an absolute authority. Now, with that concept of willingly yielding yourself by presenting yourself to a royal lord for the purpose of exercising his will, we can read the next three verses.

But thanks be to God that though you were slaves of sin, you became obedient from the heart to that form of teaching to which you were committed, and having been freed from sin, you become slaves of righteousness. I am speaking in human terms because of the weakness of your flesh. For just as you *presented* your members as slaves to impurity and to lawlessness, resulting in further lawlessness, so now *present* your members as slaves to righteousness, resulting in sanctification (Rom. 6:17–19, emphasis mine).

Do you get the picture? Paul is not saying be righteous and you will feel righteous. He is saying to submit to being a slave, a servant, a soldier, and give your allegiance to your master and king as an act of your will.

But there's a problem. What do you do when you are called upon to obey and you have no power to obey? This touches on an area that until now we haven't dealt with thoroughly: the ministry of the Holy Spirit. The Holy Spirit is available to you now to empower you for daily, victorious living. It isn't enough merely to have information. We need the ministry of the Holy Spirit to apply practically in our lives what God says is true of us.*

In chapter 7 of the Book of Romans, Paul says there was a time in his life that he wanted to obey the law of God but he lacked the power to do it (vv. 18–25). Why? Paul had not then been raised to new life by the power of the Holy Spirit. He could not obey even when he had the desire to obey. How do you appropriate the power of the Holy Spirit in your life? The answer is simple but profound: by faith. And this is where faith and commitment are joined. When we consciously choose to obey, the Holy Spirit responds to that desire and empowers us to carry out God's will. Sometimes we have no other motivation to obey than the sheer commitment to the

---

* See Appendix for a more complete discussion of the importance of the Holy Spirit in empowering you for joy-filled living.

principle of obedience. And then we must walk in the power of the Holy Spirit by faith.

Faith has a two-pronged meaning: "to live out" and "in accordance with." So to truly believe, one must choose to live in accordance with that belief. Obedience is incorporated into what biblical faith actually means. Believing is not mere mental consent; the root meaning of faith includes action. Belief leads naturally to action. That which the mind accepts the will must obey, otherwise you are not really a believer. A believer of a truth will naturally follow his belief into action. Obedience is nothing more than faith in action.

When I joined Campus Crusade for Christ twenty years ago, my ambition was to be a traveling youth speaker. There was already one traveling speaker for Crusade at that time, and he made it very clear to me that there was room for only one. It was a source of irritation to him that I believed various teachings of his were unbiblical and detrimental to the cause of Christ. Some time later, when I would not cooperate with an unauthorized policy that I knew Dr. Bright, the director, was opposed to, a few in leadership positions, including my irritated superior, found a way to remove me. Placement time came. I had been promised an assignment under the high school director to travel as a speaker in the High School Ministry. It was an opportunity I had waited for. Unknown to Dr. Bright, those brothers in leadership assigned me to Argentina. It was either go or leave the staff of Crusade.

I was shocked and hurt by this news. It was an attempt to remove me from the scene because I was a threat. Struggling with feelings of resentment, I thought, "How can they get away with this?" And then I remembered Rom. 6:19: "present your members as slaves to righteousness, resulting in sanctification." I was tempted to "fight" this assignment by going to Dr. Bright with the problem. But I also remembered Heb. 13:17: "Obey your leaders, and submit to them; for they keep watch over your souls, as those who will give an account. Let them do this with joy and not with grief, for this would be unprofitable to you." I believed God wanted me to return blessing for insult. In obedience I willingly submitted to the Argentina assignment.

Now, I didn't have the power to keep from resenting the person who had caused this injustice. But in response to my obedience God the Holy Spirit took control of my emotions. I had a peace and contentment about my assignment, and I sensed God's warm personal approval of me. Oh, I was being rejected all right, and it hurt, but the momentary injustice couldn't overshadow the sense of acceptance I had from God.

Obedience opens the door for the Holy Spirit to apply to your emotions what in reality you are in Christ. Acting your way into right feelings is always the right order. Experience the peace and joy of your salvation by fixing your mind on what is true of you in Christ, responding to His will in your life. Live according to who God says you are, not according to your feelings.

If you have been mistreated lately or had someone reject you, drop on your knees to Christ, submit to the abuse and mistreatment, and call upon the power of the Holy Spirit for a righteous response. You can't produce a right response on your own—don't try. That comes through the power of the Spirit. Concentrate on presenting yourself as a servant to God and confessing your need for His power. He is there to live through you.

Faith in God is the key that unlocks the secret to your feeling accepted. Don't make it more complicated than it is. Don't look to yourself or your failures for excuses to not believe God's view of you. Don't let Satan convince you you're not who God says you are. Look to God with faith. He's your object of trust. Believe Him for who He is—a God who loves you and accepts you because of Christ's death, resurrection, and seating on your behalf. Believe what He says is true and rest in it—you'll find true acceptance.

7

A Case for Insecurity

There are more single parent homes in our society today than there have ever been. Single parents, particularly, face pressures most others never face. Loneliness, heartache, and insecurity hang like a pall over the lives of many modern sophisticates. People grasp for any hope to ease the gnawing emptiness and gripping anxiety inside—from momentary escape to suicide.

LISA'S STORY

By the time a young woman named Lisa came for counsel she was confused about the direction of her life and shaken in her faith. She had recently experienced a tragic and painful divorce; facing each day required courage. The divorce settlement required that she and her former husband sell the house for which they had worked so hard. But under the circumstances she had been glad that the house sold quickly. With her share of the money, Lisa found an adequate apartment for herself and the two children. She was still confronted with the difficult prospect of raising her seven-year-old son and five-year-old daughter alone, as well as the task of finding a new job. As a fairly new Christian she was doing her best to remain faithful to Christ, but her circumstances conspired against her fledgling belief.

Her job hunting turned into a full-time occupation, the days stretching on into weeks. The money from the house sale was dwindling. She *had* to find a job! Where was God when she needed Him most?

Just as her faith threatened to collapse, she got a job. Not a terribly high-paying one, but a job.

The pressure was temporarily relieved, and then she had

a car accident. Her car, which sustained minor damage, was drivable, but the other was damaged extensively, and she was responsible for its repair. Because of her financial status, with the rent to pay, and grocery, utility, telephone, gasoline, and other bills coming in, Lisa had not been able to keep up her insurance premiums. She just didn't have the money to repair the other car. What would she do?

Only hours after her accident a call came from Chad's school. The school office had discovered Lisa's move to a new school district, and her son Chad had to transfer within a week! Lisa had so hoped that he could finish up the school year at his old school. Uprooting Chad from the security of familiar surroundings, after losing a father, a home, and every other stable thing in his life, seemed totally unjust. But the school authorities wouldn't listen to reason. They had their code to abide by. Chad was crushed. He didn't want to go to another school and leave his friends and teacher; he didn't know anyone in the other school. He cried all evening. Lately, her little daughter had been waking up nights sobbing for her daddy, too. That night the children, after being comforted by their mother, finally gave in to sleep, but there was neither comfort nor sleep for Lisa.

Lisa had lost any sense of security. "Where is God?" she asked. "Doesn't He see what is happening? Why doesn't He help?"

Lisa needed to know that God had not lost control of her world. She needed the assurance that what was taking place would eventually be used for her good and for God's glory.

Many well-meaning Christians tried to comfort Lisa by reiterating that God would take care of her. They never accompanied their advice, though, with reasons why she should believe that. Lisa had been trying to hold onto a faith that believed God would come through for her, because, in her words, "God said He'd take care of me, and I believe Him." But now under the pressures of her trials, Lisa's belief in God as her protector and provider had reached the breaking point.

So often security eludes us. Life seems so uncertain. We all long for that inner stability and confidence that enables us to be content when life's trials come. We *want* to be free of anxiety that causes ulcers and turns us into bundles of nerves.

In the two previous sections we discovered the connections between faith and love and between faith and self-acceptance. Now we want to examine the relationship of faith to security. By faith we can have that security we so desire, unlocking the secret to knowing *why* God can be trusted, whatever our circumstances.

LISA'S PERSPECTIVE

Lisa felt confused and insecure. She questioned God's promise to provide for her. She didn't want to be bitter about her trying circumstances, but it was hard to keep from fearing what would happen to her and her children.

LISA'S NEED

Lisa needed that easiness of mind and heart that is security. She needed some evidence that God would deliver (or was delivering) on His promise to care for her even when it looked as if He wasn't.

LISA'S "SOLUTION"

"The only thing I know to do is keep hoping God will answer my prayers," Lisa said. "I don't know what else to do." Lisa looked to God to bail her out, because she believed, after all, that God loved her and wanted to help her.

But that's only half the story. Lisa did not see the complete picture. In light of what Lisa knew about God, her faith had little to hold onto.

Yes, she believed God would provide and protect her because God was just and loving. And that's true; He would. But there's another dimension to God's faithfulness: not only God's loving intentions, but His perfect ability. Remember?

In chapter two, we mentioned two qualities about God that give us a reason to trust Him: His perfect character and unfailing performance. Evidence about God provides the basis on which to believe in complete confidence that He cares and will meet needs.

TWO KINDS OF FAITH

Lisa needed evidence to support her belief that God not only was willing, but was able, to meet her needs 100 percent of the time. The Christian's faith is not a blind faith, but an intelligent faith. It must have reasons to believe in God's perfect character and unfailing performance, or it will soon grow weary under the avalanche of adversity and circumstances that seem to say, "God doesn't care." Evidence of God's control will assure you, though the circumstances tell you differently, that God will supply your needs. You'll be able to say, "Here's the reason I believe that," and stand firm in life's most troubling times. Taking the principle of faith based on evidence (which everyone needs in order to believe in Christ), and applying it to the need for security creates a deep sense of contentment and joy. Faith needs substance to qualify as true, biblical faith.

Intelligent, knowledgeable faith is an exercise of trust evaluated by the mind, confirmed with the heart, and based upon adequate evidence or information. Simply "having faith" is not enough. Faith must be accompanied by convictions—convictions based on sufficient biblical knowledge, facts, and evidence. A person without a knowledgeable faith will invariably suffer fear, anxiety, and basic insecurity. That's why the Bible so strongly urges us to study and to learn God's plan and purpose through His Word (1 Tim. 2:15).

We don't have to demand evidence. God has already provided evidence for His trustworthiness. All we have to do is examine it. Jesus went so far as to say: "If I do not do the works of My Father, do not believe Me; but if I do them, though you do not believe Me, believe the works, that you may know and understand that the Father is in Me, and I in the Father" (John 10:37–38).

Christ invites you to investigate His works, His performance, that support His claim to be God. But notice where He intends your investigation to lead—"that you may know (continually know) and understand" who He really is. Christ wants your examination of the evidence to be an examination of *Him*. Getting to know the kind of God you serve will naturally engender trust.

The motivation in asking you to examine the evidence is not to create a "rationalistic faith" or an "intellectual" approach to Christianity. Examining evidence for faith is an adventure into a personal acquaintance with the character and ability of Jesus Christ. God wants you to know Him and to know that He is in complete control of all of life's circumstances. "Seek Me early and you shall find Me," "Ask and it shall be given, seek and ye shall find, knock and it shall be opened unto you." As you seek to know why God is not only willing, but very able, to meet every need, the Holy Spirit will enable you to rest secure in His plan for your life.

But the vital evidence that is to ground your faith must be gathered and examined. Where is the evidence that God can be trusted? How do you know that He will come through on His promises 100 percent of the time? One must gather the facts about God's faithfulness in the past to substantiate whether He always meets needs. As a result you will be encouraged to believe God more, understanding that He meets the needs of His people, even if for the moment the situation seems otherwise. If Lisa would weigh all the evidence, she would know beyond any reasonable doubt that God fulfills His promises. That means that whatever your trying circumstance may be, there is substantial evidence that gives you a basis for joy, even in the face of any momentary crisis. You could lose a job and feel secure—lose a loved one and feel secure—lose a home and feel secure—lose a relationship and feel secure. What a mind-boggling prospect to pursue!

8

Unlocking the Secret to Security

When Christ declares, "Trust me, I've got everything under control," He doesn't say that in a vacuum. He says that amidst the storms of interruptions, irritations, ill treatment, disease, disaster, and death, against the backdrop of His faithfulness and trustworthiness. Lisa is a modern-day example of the "wonderer," wondering if God had forgotten her, deserted her, left her stranded. But God hadn't forgotten Lisa, and He doesn't forget about you and me.

God's Word gives us insight into the balance we need in using intelligent faith. Intelligent faith doesn't mean we'll understand everything. We will not always know what God is doing in a time of pain, or heartbreak, or a bewildering series of setbacks. But intelligent faith decides to believe God, and bases that trust on knowledge of the Scriptures; evidence about God's unquestioned ability to control the events of history and people's lives in times past—especially in the lives of biblical characters.

SECURITY IN GOD'S CONTROL

The Bible gives us an abundance of evidence that God controls history. The Bible is genuine, recorded testimony of God's involvement in history. God is God who "acts." When doubts assail our belief in God's sovereignty, intelligent knowledgeable faith returns again and again to the ample evidence of His absolute dominion in the Scriptures. As we peer into the lives of men and women as revealed in God's Word, those who experienced God's sovereign control in their lives, we gain confidence and certainty that God will do the same for us. In this sense, the Bible is God's track record. God has given us a compendium of instruction concerning

Himself through the history of His interaction with His people.

The Apostle Paul instructed the Corinthian church (and they needed instruction) on this very point. In two different places in the same chapter the Apostle drives home the preeminent point of the Old Testament: *"Now these things happened as examples for us, that we should not crave evil things, as they also craved"* (1 Cor. 10:6, emphasis mine). And again: *"Now these things happened to them as an example, and they were written for our instruction,* upon whom the ends of the ages have come" (1 Cor. 10:11, emphasis mine).

Notice in your Bible the number of historical incidents the Apostle recounts in 1 Cor. 10:1–12 from the pages of the Old Testament:

- Israel's being led by the pillar and cloud
- The crossing of the Red Sea
- God's provision of manna
- Moses striking the rock for water
- Israel's unbelief at not crossing into Canaan
- Israel's idolatry in worshiping the golden calf
- The erection of the bronze serpent to save the Israelites from poisonous snakes
- Korah's rebellion against Moses

All these incidents demonstrate God's involvement in the lives of His people and His ultimate sovereignty. Equally, the histories of Joseph, Samson, David, Gideon, Job, and Daniel—in fact, everything in the Old Testament—were given for us to see the hand of a sovereign God working in people's lives.

I think the hymn writer who penned these words got the point:

> O God, our help in ages past,
> Our hope for years to come,
> Be Thou our Guide while life shall last,
> And our Eternal Home.

The next time you sing "O God, Our Help in Ages Past," think of 1 Cor. 10:1–12 and rest secure in God's control. Based on the record of God's faithfulness in the past, you can confidently submit to His control both now and in the future.

The feast of Passover is one of the most meaningful traditions in the home life of a Jewish family. The family patriarch recites to the members of the family at the time of the Passover meal the remarkable acts of God in calling His people out of Egyptian slavery into the promised land. Dottie and I have attempted to revive the principle of this ancient practice in our home. During breakfast, I will either read or relate a Bible story to my children, not simply to acquaint them with the facts of the historical event, but to acquaint them with a faithful God and His ability to care for His people. I want to teach my children of God's wisdom, love, authority, righteous judgment, and power. And I know that the more my children learn of Him through history, the more they'll be able to trust Him based on their knowledge of His character and ability.

The premier example of God's ultimate power and control of events in the New Testament is Christ's resurrection. Repeatedly the Apostles pointed to the resurrection as demonstrative of Christ's kingship over life. In other words (not to be irreverent but to make the point), if God can pull that off, don't worry about what you're facing! It's peanuts compared to what God did in raising Jesus Christ from the dead.

You might be saying, "Why don't I feel secure?" For the same reason, no doubt, that Lisa felt insecure—you may be focusing on the immediate circumstances surrounding you rather than resting in God's total sovereignty. Oh, how your loving heavenly Father wants you to look at the evidence of His control in history and His ability to manage men's affairs. He wants you to trust Him, to believe that *He* is in control and that no circumstances can alter His plan for your life.

TRUSTING IN GOD'S CONTROL

Based on the evidence of history and God's involvement in men's lives, we must affirm our trust in God's control. That's not the same, however, as *feeling* that God is in control. The two don't necessarily go together. But by acting on the facts you know about God from the Scripture, and what you know to be true of God's sovereign control, the feelings will follow. One of the greatest expressions of faith is not asking "Why?" but "For what purpose?" God knows what is going to happen before it happens, and He plans to use it for your good and His glory. Your trust in God's control can lead you to say, like Job, "He knows the way that I take" (Job 23:10). And we can add to that, "Even if for the moment I don't."

You must realize your mind can't comprehend or know what God knows. Have you ever seen the Norman Rockwell painting of the little boy watching a baseball game through a knothole in the ballpark fence? The boy's line of sight is straight ahead. Anything to one side is out of his field of vision; anything close up is obscured. The spectators in the stands, of course, see the whole game. Your view of life is like the boy's—extremely limited. In contrast, God sees "the whole game." God sees the beginning and the end of time at once, and therefore, He holds within His mind the eternal pattern of His creation's meaning.

So what does an intelligent faith in God's control do when faced with circumstances or ill-meaning people who challenge that control? Intelligent faith examines the evidence, looks over God's track record, we might say, and decides that God has not lost control. God knows what's happening, and He is in control working out His will. *You* may not know *what* God knows, but you do know *that* He knows.

IDENTIFYING A PROPER RESPONSE

Once you affirm your faith in God's control, then you need to ask yourself, "How does God's Word direct me to act in this crisis? What should be my reaction when trials and persecutions come my way?"

God's Word gives you the answer. Listen to God's spirit through Peter:

> Beloved, do not be surprised at the fiery ordeal among you, which comes upon you for your testing [testing of faith], as though some strange thing were happening to you; but to the degree that you share the sufferings of Christ, keep on rejoicing; so that also at the revelation of His glory, you may rejoice with exultation. If you are reviled for the name of Christ, you are blessed, because the Spirit of glory and of God rests upon you. By no means let any of you suffer as a murderer, or thief, or evildoer, or a troublesome meddler; . . . Therefore, let those also who suffer according to the will of God entrust their souls to a faithful Creator in doing what is right (1 Pet. 4:12–19).

Let's summarize the response we've examined in previous chapters:

1. Expect testing. Don't be surprised by trials and tribulations. The righteous do suffer. And God's Word teaches us to expect it: Christ, after all, wasn't spared the horror of crucifixion. He is the premier example of the righteous one who suffers unjustly (1 Pet. 3:18).

2. Keep rejoicing. God knows it is unnatural to be glad when trials swoop down upon you. So, He encourages you to rejoice. Rejoicing in the testing changes your outlook and attitude. You can begin to believe God again!—

particularly if you know trials are instruments God uses (as He uses all things) for your good and His glory.

3. Do what is right. God wants your response, in both attitude and actions, to be in accordance with His character. As James writes, "Who among you is wise and understanding? Let him show by his good behavior his deeds in the gentleness of wisdom. . . . The wisdom from above is first pure, then peaceable, gentle, reasonable, full of mercy and good fruits, unwavering, without hypocrisy" (3:13, 17). Allow God's Word to mold your mind, shape your attitudes, and dominate your responses. Learn new patterns of thinking—Christlike patterns—and you will experience the joy of surmounting your obstacles.

SEEKING A PURPOSE FROM GOD'S WORD

After affirming God's sovereignty and identifying your proper response, you must seek God's purpose in your difficulties. But, you may object, didn't you just say that we can't know all the reasons, the whys for what takes place? Yes, but you can discern God's overall purpose for trials, which supplies even more evidence on which to base your faith.

GRACE FOR DEVELOPMENT
IN CHRISTLIKENESS

We can speak of three basic modes of experiencing purpose and meaning in the midst of trials and persecutions.

God said He causes all things to work together for your good, remember? He went on to identify that good. "For whom He foreknew, He also predestined to become conformed to the image of His Son, that He might be the firstborn among many brethren" (Rom. 8:29).

One of God's purposes in trials is to use them to provide grace for molding you into the likeness of Christ. Seeing trials from that perspective makes all the difference in the world. God plans to use the circumstances of your daily experience to develop you in a specific direction. The "good" God wants to bring about in you is a specific good, not just generally good things. It is to specifically bring you into conformity with the character of Jesus Christ.

Patience is not my strong suit, I'll admit. But God is in the process of developing that virtue in my life; I know because I find myself far too many times painfully aware of its lack.

On one occasion when I had a very important speaking engagement in Denver, there was a need to rent a large screen for a media presentation that accompanied my address. The screen was ordered from San Francisco, and it was to be sent to Denver, and billed to my office. But because of a clerical error in San Francisco, the rental company shipped the screen to my office and the bill to Denver. When I arrived in Denver the night before my lecture, there was a phone message waiting from my office: "Where are we supposed to put the 15' × 20' screen you ordered?"

Now, without that screen, it would be difficult to give my lecture. If I didn't give my lecture, six months of planning, promotion, and organization by the local sponsors would go up in smoke, not to mention the money invested. And then, there were the over 3,300 people who had registered for the conference to consider.

The more I considered how the San Francisco screen company had bungled the order, the angrier I got. While I said nothing to anyone about my unhappiness, I felt the frustration rising. Why couldn't anyone get things straight?

When I got to my room I sat down and set out on another course of thinking. Who knew where the screen would be before it ever got there? Who ultimately controlled all the shipping companies? And who was I lecturing for in the first place? I began to think of God's sovereignty over my speaking engagements, my traveling, and over media screens. I prayed and told the Lord that this was His conference and if He wanted me to speak with a screen, without a screen, or not speak at all, it was in His care.

As I reached for the phone to call and see what could be done, I thought of words like *rejoice, gentleness,* and *kindness.* Those were not the words in my mind five minutes earlier! But now I was bringing to mind what my response *should be.* I sat back in my chair and meditated. God has a purpose here, I mused. I'm not sure if He wants to cancel my meeting or not. But I know He wants me to be like Him. He desires that I "suffer long and be kind," that I have the virtue of patience. I lifted my thoughts to God in praise for His interest in me, for controlling and ordering the steps of my life. The more I praised Him, the more I rested my case in His care. I called my office and asked them to send the screen to me by air freight. It arrived at the Denver airport early that next morning, the morning of the conference. The San Francisco firm apologized for the inconvenience and paid for the air freight charges. The conference went on as planned.

All our problems don't always end happily like that, and I don't always respond to a situation the same way. But the principle is the same. God desires to restore us to complete Christlikeness, and our faith is the force that unleashes God's grace for growth.

Two key words in the passage from Rom. 8:29 need to be highlighted: *conformed* and *image.*

Conformed signifies an inward, essential change of character. *Conformed* comes from the same root word used in Rom. 12:2 where it's translated *transformed:* "And do not be conformed [not the same word] to this world, but be *transformed* [the same word: signifying an inward change of character] by the renewing of your mind, that you may prove what the will of God is, that which is good and acceptable and perfect." The word translated as either "conformed" or "transformed" comes from the Greek *metamorphoō.* Scientists get the word *metamorphosis* from this Greek word, which describes the total transformation a caterpillar undergoes in changing into a butterfly.

Image comes from the word for a statue. It's important to note that a statue is three-dimensional. In Greek, a photograph, being two-dimensional, would require the word for a *"likeness,"* while only a sculpture could be identified with the word the Greeks use for a *representation*. When the Greeks spoke of a representation they had in mind the highest possible degree of imitation in another form.

Paul says God's plan is to change us into "an exact representation of Christ." One fine expositor comments on the Apostle's wording: "believers are . . . to represent, not something like Him, but what He is in Himself, both in His spiritual body and in His moral character."

We may be reminded, in this regard, of Paul's words regarding the process of the believer becoming like Christ: "But we all, with unveiled face beholding as in a mirror the glory of the Lord, are being transformed [inward, essential change of character] into the same image [exact representation] from glory to glory, just as from the Lord, the Spirit" (2 Cor. 3:18).

The process of becoming Christlike is accomplished by the indwelling presence of the Holy Spirit. You are being made into a new person, a part of God's new race, with Christ as the head of that new nation. But this is a process; we're statues now, but one day we will undergo a complete metamorphosis, and "this mortal shall put on immortality."

With his characteristic wit, C. S. Lewis says regarding the process of our change into Christlikeness: "And that is what Christianity is all about. This world is a great sculptor's shop. We are the statues and there is a rumor going round the shop that some of us are some day going to come to life."

But let me confess, I do not always know what areas of my life God desires to perfect in me. As I continue to yield to God's hand in each circumstance and respond properly, He continues to fashion in me the character qualities of Jesus. While I don't always know the specific quality God wants to develop in me, there is at least one quality that seems to fit if another doesn't. Paul, the Apostle, identified this quality as the one God was fashioning in him when he didn't get an answer to his prayer for God to remove his "thorn in the flesh." While I am not certain what the thorn was, I know it was a trial to him. He had asked three times that God remove his thorn. The only reply he received from God was: "My grace is sufficient for you, for power is perfected in weakness" (2 Cor. 12:9).

What was God's purpose in the thorn other than to tell Paul He had grace for him to endure it? If for no other reason, it would serve to keep him humble: "lest I should be exalted above measure through the abundance of the revelations" (2 Cor. 12:7, KJV). Paul had been privileged to have insights into spiritual truth that others had not had. He perceived his thorn would keep him from exalting himself. That was sufficient for Paul. He didn't have to look any further for a purpose in his trial. His final attitude was: "Therefore I am well content with weaknesses, with insults, with distresses, with persecutions, with difficulties, for Christ's sake" (2 Cor. 12:10). So if you can find no other reason for a trial, you can recognize it, with Paul, as a means by which God is drawing you closer to Him, and accept it in meekness as a lesson in humility.

That is probably, of course, the hardest test of all. But things as great in themselves as the test is difficult can come of it. Hannah W. Smith captures the essence of the Spirit's work in conforming a young woman to the image of Christ:

> The circumstances of her life she could not alter, but she took them to the Lord, and handed them over into His management; and then she believed that He took it, and she left all the responsibility and the worry and anxiety with Him. . . . And the result was that, although the circumstances remained unchanged, her soul was kept in perfect peace in the midst of them. And the secret she found so effectual in her outward affairs, she

found to be still more effectual in her inward ones, which were in truth even more utterly unmanageable. She abandoned her whole self to the Lord, with all that she was and all that she had; and, believing that He took that which she had committed to Him, she ceased to fret and worry, and her life became all sunshine in the gladness of belonging to Him.

GRACE FOR EFFECTIVE SERVICE

Trials not only provide us with the opportunity to be more complete, mature people, but they also provide us the opportunity to minister to others. They give us the empathy with which to comfort others. Have you ever said to someone, "I know how you must feel," and then later thought you couldn't possibly have known how that person had felt because you never had gone through that kind of ordeal? Well, often God allows you to go through times when you don't feel loved by some loved ones, when you're rejected by friends, when some of your "security blankets" are removed, in order to provide grace for the purpose of making you more effective in ministry to others.

I can say I know what it feels like to lose a mother, who was my bellwether. I know what it's like to suffer the tragic loss of a sister by cancer. God comforted me through all that. And I have the opportunity to say in all truth to others who have lost loved ones, "I know how you feel. I've been there too."

Do you remember I shared with you my ambition to be a traveling youth speaker with Campus Crusade? Let me give the second half of that story. Without Dr. Bright's knowledge or approval some people in leadership assigned me to Argentina. It was either go or leave the staff of Crusade. I was tempted to "fight" this assignment by going over their heads to Dr. Bright with the problem. Instead I felt restrained and remembered that God had called me to minister with Crusade, and He knew in advance that the leadership wasn't

97

perfect. I left for South America with knots in my stomach and reservations in my mind. Were these men wrong in shipping me off to Argentina? Was God really in control? However, even though I could not understand why this was happening to me, my two years in Latin America were precisely what I needed, and God knew it. The experience equipped me with skills in university debates and the free speech lectures.

After God had sufficiently prepared me in spirit and mind, Dr. Bright learned of my situation and the events that led to my South American assignment. He felt the time was ripe for a work in the states similar to my university speaking ministry in South America. The group of men who had sent me into "exile" were now gone. Dr. Bright immediately called me home. From that call, my national university lecture ministry was born. While a few misguided men meant to remove me, God meant to prepare me. I learned how God uses circumstances and trials as stepping stones to more effective ways of ministry service.

THE PRESENCE OF COMFORT

I've heard others say, in an attempt to comfort someone in trouble, "Well, it will all work out." They seem to imply that God mixes the ingredients of disappointment and sorrow up in His celestial batter, and we will only learn the proof of His intentions in this heavenly pudding long after the events which caused the pain are past.

There is some truth to that. But always looking away to some distant future may well obscure what God is doing in your life *now!* Look again at Rom. 8:28. The New American Standard Bible translates it: "And we know that *God causes* all things to work out for good" (my emphasis). In the original there is an emphasis on the words *all things.* The implication is that God is at work in every single event of your life to bring about your good. He doesn't overlook a single detail.

That's not to say that God regards or that you should

regard everything in itself as good. The results of sin, selfishness, and perversion are *not* good. God only promises to work *through* each thing in your life. No matter what its original character, if you offer it up to Him, He can use it as a tool in carving out "the good" in you.

Remember Lisa? How does a knowledgeable faith help Lisa in her trying circumstances? She couldn't, for the moment, see how any good would come out of her plight. I counseled Lisa to weigh all the evidence in light of her trying circumstances. It might *not* look as if God was in control or had her best interest at heart, but the weight of evidence of history would bear out the validity of His promise in Rom. 8:28. She could rest secure, by an act of intelligent faith, in God's control.

I have to be honest with you and report that Lisa failed. The others, Karen and Dan, and Mike and Sue, took creative steps to restoration with God. Lisa, however, neglected to seriously examine the evidence regarding God's control. Her faith lacked substance, and her hopes faded. She never experienced security in the knowledge that God was working out His will in her life. Today she is a bitter, resentful, tortured woman, eaten by the haunting memories of the past. The choice was hers.

We too have a choice.

9

A Story of God's Faithfulness

To conclude our search in unlocking the secrets of being loved, accepted, and secure, I would like to share a period of my life that I believe illustrates how all three needs are met by faith in a God who is faithful, righteous, and all-powerful.

Have you ever experienced the pain of breaking a long-term dating relationship or engagement? You will remember my mentioning in an earlier chapter that in the early years of my Campus Crusade ministry I dated a wonderful woman for three and a half years. I shared there that I loved Paula and thought she was everything I ever wanted in a wife. She was spiritually in tune with God, intelligent, articulate, gentle, and sincere. And best of all, she loved *me* and thought I was everything she wanted in a husband. We began to talk of marriage.

While directing the Campus Crusade for Christ work in Canada, God began to show me that He was going to take Paula out of my life because she was not the woman for me. Paula and I both were plagued with nagging doubts about our relationship; she told me later that she too struggled with a distinct lack of peace about our relationship but could not put her finger on the problem. But each of us hid our doubts for fear of hurting the other. Finally the turmoil became so intense that I had to share it with Paula.

I traveled down the West Coast on a speaking tour and stopped over to see her in San Diego. After I had spoken at one of the fraternities at San Diego State, Paula and I went out to a Mexican restaurant in old town San Diego. We both sensed what was coming but did not want to face it. Finally, I smiled weakly and said, "Well . . . what do you think?"

Paula burst into tears. "Oh, Josh, I feel awful," she sobbed. Seeing her in tears brought me to tears as well, and I realized that God did not want us together. We decided to break off the engagement and wait and see if our feelings about God's will would change. We knew that if God wanted us together, nothing could keep us apart. That night we drove to Balboa Park and walked in the night air. It was so strange! We both knew clearly that we were not to marry, yet we felt so close and dear to each other. We walked and talked until two o'clock in the morning, reminiscing over the fun times we had had and the things we had learned together about God.

The next morning Paula and her mother picked me up at my motel and took me to the airport. I stayed composed the whole time, acting as if I wasn't bothered by the breakup at all. How I hated to leave, but I knew I couldn't stay. Kissing Paula good-bye was like kissing my future good-bye. It seemed as if all my hopes and dreams of marriage and a family that I had secretly nurtured were shattered, destroyed, dead.

It was a long agonizing walk from the door of the terminal to the plane. I swore to myself that I'd never go through such a heartache again. It was such a temptation to turn around, run back, throw my arms around Paula, and say, "Let's get married. I'll forget about Christian work. I'll go back to law school, I'll get a functional degree, start a functional practice, we'll get a functional house, have functional kids, and just function."

I literally pulled myself up the steps to the plane and, upon reaching the door, began to cry. A stewardess carried my attaché bag and led me to my seat. It was one of the most difficult times of my life, and I came perilously close to cursing God and turning my back on Him. My thoughts screamed, "Why, God? You say You're a God of love? How could You take the only true love I ever had out of my life? It isn't right to be denied love. God, You can't love me and do this to me!"

Sitting on the plane, I felt my whole world was caving in. I was convinced God was angry with me and was punishing me. It seemed that He didn't want me to experience true love and didn't really care if I was ever happy.

After a couple of hours my emotions subsided and God began to work. He reminded me, "For God so loved the world that He gave His only Son"; "All things work together for good"; "I will withhold no good thing from those that walk uprightly." I began to quiet down and say, "God, I love You. I know You've called me to the ministry. And You're not taking Paula from my life because You want to punish me, but rather because You love me and have a plan for my life. You want my life to be filled with the greatest joy. It still hurts, God, but I accept Your will for me. If Paula is not to be my wife, then I know You have a better plan for Paula and a better plan for me."

Right then taking a giant step of faith, I said, "God, lead on. I want to follow Your design for my life. By faith I give my future into Your hands. You have something better for me, not necessarily better than Paula, but better for *me* than Paula." What a lesson to learn, that God sometimes has to pry us loose from the good to give us the best.

The decision to submit myself to God's will and accept His plan for my life was made easier because of knowing *why* I believed. Trusting a God who loved me and who had proved His love for me in numerous ways was very helpful. He not only had saved me and given me purpose and fellowship with Him, but He had supplied all my needs and most of my wants. He had miraculously supplied my financial needs on several occasions; had brought me into a ministry-team relationship with a group of men and women whom I dearly loved; had enriched my life through Paula's friendship and challenge to serve Christ; had provided me, through Paula's mom and dad, a model of Christian parents I'd never had at home; had blessed me with all spiritual blessings in Christ; and had my life's plan and future all under control. If He had done all of this in the past, I reasoned, surely He can do something even greater in the future. I was beginning to climb out of the pit.

My faith in God wasn't blind. I was taking the facts I knew about a faithful, loving God and relating them to my will and damaged emotions. God had not only been faithful in my life, but in Paula's life as well. God had been faithful to men and women whom I knew of throughout history, and I had the record of Bible characters who had experienced God's trustworthiness. I reminded myself of the historical evidence regarding the identity, life, death, and resurrection of Christ that was so forceful in bringing me to a decision for Christ. Even in a situation in which God seemed to be nowhere near, because I could look back on all the evidence of God's love, concern, faithfulness, and trustworthiness, I knew *why* I could trust my heavenly Father.

At the time that it was clear God was taking Paula away from me, I cried, "Why, God? What have I done to deserve this? Have I sinned? Are You punishing me for something I've done?"

I felt the worst kind of rejection—rejection by God. I thought for some reason God found me unacceptable, that He was punishing me by taking Paula out of my life. I tried to make deals with God. "O God, if I pray longer and harder, can I have her back? If I go to church more, will You give her back to me? If I study my Bible more, will You let me have her then? I'll do anything to find Your favor again, God." I thought God was mad at me, that He was punishing me. Therefore, I thought, if I performed to please God He would give me what I wanted.

But the more I learn about God the greater confidence I have for trusting Him. If Christ is God as He claims to be and as the Bible teaches that He is, then He is able to accomplish what He said He would accomplish: my acceptance with Him. I can't improve my standing with God by religious performance, prayer, Bible reading or church attendance. My acceptance with God is already won for me in Christ. God wasn't rejecting me by withholding something wonderful from me. He was fulfilling His loving intentions toward me as my heavenly Father by giving me something better later, rather than allowing me to settle for less now.

One reason I reacted so strongly against giving up Paula was my mistaken notion that she was my last hope of love in this world. I wanted love; I needed love; and I erroneously focused my attention on a human relationship as my ultimate source of love.

Remember the first concept that Christianity is a relationship, not a religion? That relationship with God is the starting point to find love, for I will never be separated from God's love. As I acquaint myself with Him, with His character and nature as a God of love, and reflect on His eternal display of love—His death on the cross—I am reminded that I am loved by an eternal, unstoppable, unconditional love.

My faith was tested the most when I doubted God's control of my life. It was difficult to believe that a loving God would be so cruel as to rip from me the one security I had of a future of happiness and fulfillment. I had to learn that my security was in God. Because God had demonstrated His control of events within history as revealed in Scripture and had been faithful to me over and over again, I was able to commit my future to a God who loved me, had my best interests at heart, and had the power to accomplish His will. Confidence in the Scriptures and a knowledge of His faithfulness in the past gave me an intelligent basis on which to submit my future into His hands.

It often takes time to appreciate how God works things out in our lives. Six or seven years later, when I met Dottie, I began to see how God's plan was being unfolded in my life. Even now, after eighteen years of marriage, I'm learning new dimensions of God's faithfulness. Surrounded now by a loving wife and three children, I am reminded that God loves me, Christ has won God's acceptance of me, and God is my total security in life. I now have a greater basis on which to trust God than ever before, as well as a greater basis to encourage others to trust God.

There will be times when you don't feel loved by those around you. You may feel that way now. There will be times when people reject you. And sure, life will seem topsy-turvy at times. But remember, based on what you know about God, His character and His faithfulness as an all-powerful God, you can claim the reality of the love, acceptance, and security you have in Him by faith.

ACTION STEPS TO TAKE

How can you develop a greater confidence in God, His trustworthiness and faithfulness, and His loving intentions to meet all your needs for love, acceptance, and security? There are some practical steps you can take.

1. Study the Scriptures. This should seem obvious, but most Christians don't realize the valuable library of instruction on God's faithfulness that the Bible contains. Strengthen your confidence in God by studying especially the lives of Old and New Testament men and women who experienced firsthand God's greatness, mercy, wisdom, and control. Also study the Evidence Growth Guide series, which investigates God's dealings with many Old Testament men and women. Get acquainted with the pattern of how God worked through people's lives.

2. Read Christian biographies. Purchase and read the stories of men and women who experienced God's faithfulness. Your faith will be encouraged. Here are a few biographies that have been meaningful to me:

Joni. The story of Joni Eareckson and how God gave her abundant joy in the face of total paralysis.

The Hiding Place. The story of Corrie Ten Boom and God's faithfulness in a German prison camp.

J. Hudson Taylor. A gripping story of a man's commitment to reach the world for Christ and God's trustworthiness in answer to prayer.

Thirty Years with the South Sea Cannibals. The experience of missionary John G. Patton as he reached lost men and women in out-of-the-way places for Christ.

Shadow of the Almighty. The challenging life and testament of Jim Elliott, who gave his life as a martyr for Christ in carrying the Gospel to the headhunting Auca Indians.

3. Interview mature Christians. There are many modern-day examples of God's faithfulness right near you, in your home, your church, your family, and among your friends. I encourage you to ask questions and talk to others about how God has honored His Word in their lives. You'll be motivated to trust God more as you see God working in the lives of those you know personally.

4. Be sure you're filled with the Spirit. The indwelling presence of the Holy Spirit is God's resource for bringing home to your life lessons on God's faithfulness. God's Spirit will empower you to trust more, believe more, and live supernaturally as you appropriate His power by faith. I urge you, if you have not made the discovery of being filled with the Holy Spirit by faith, don't stop here, but read the Appendix that follows, take the step that I did, and appropriate the resources that are already yours through God's Spirit.

As you take these steps, and any other creative ones I'm sure you can think of, you'll have a more intelligent faith, knowing why you trust Christ as you do, and you will personally discover God's great faithfulness and trustworthiness. As you do, you'll not only be able to trust God more in trials, but in times of success you'll know to whom to pass on the thanks.

As you've discovered, unearthing principles that profoundly affect lives requires a commitment of time and energy. Anything fresh, new, alive, and relevant demands sacrifice. Since you've read this far, apparently you understand this too. Now it's time to put this book aside and apply what you've learned. Even though you and I have probed deeply into our innermost selves through these pages, all this discussion is still theoretical. Now reality begins. Be bold. Discard your former timidity, take God at His Word, and trust Him for what He claims to be and do. You've got the groundwork laid through knowing why God can be trusted. Now you have a lifetime of opportunity to do what you say you believe.

You're in for the time of your life!

Appendix

How to Be Filled with the Holy Spirit by Faith

The most effective way to explain the wonderful discovery I made of the Spirit-filled life is to share a conversation I had with Bill Bright, director and founder of Campus Crusade for Christ.

While a student at Wheaton College, I had the opportunity to have lunch with Dr. Bright. During our time together, the conversation centered on the ministry of the inexhaustible resources available to every Christian as a result of the indwelling presence of the Holy Spirit. Dr. Bright explained that something wonderful happened to the Lord's disciples on the day of Pentecost. They were filled with the Holy Spirit and went forth in His power to change the course of history.

Dr. Bright pointed out that the same Holy Spirit who empowered the disciples to live holy lives and be powerful, fruitful witnesses wants to perform that life-changing miracle in each of our lives.

The conversation that followed completely changed my view of the Holy Spirit and the power of His indwelling presence.

"The fact," continued Bright, "that Jesus Christ lives in us and expresses His love through us is one of the most important truths in the Word of God. The standards of the Christian life are so high and so impossible to achieve that, according to the Word of God, only one person has been able to succeed. That person is Jesus Christ. When we receive Christ into our lives, we experience a new birth and we are indwelt by the Spirit. From that point on, everything we need—including wisdom, love, power—to be men and women of God and to be fruitful witnesses for Christ is available to us.

"The Christian life can be compared to the journey of a man swimming upstream against a surging current. His progress is slow and tortuous. The man can continue his attempt to swim upstream, or he can choose to board a boat with a powerful motor that can whisk him up the river effortlessly. The swimmer can always choose to get back in the water and trust his own efforts, or he can be carried along by the immeasurably more powerful boat for the completion of his journey. Such is the contrast between living the Christian life in the power of the Holy Spirit or in the energy of the flesh.

"Why do people neglect the limitless resources of the Holy Spirit and instead rely on their own efforts for living the Christian life? Many Christians are not filled—controlled and empowered—with the Spirit because of a lack of knowledge. They are fruitless and powerless simply because they do not know how to experience the power of the Holy Spirit.

"Josh," Dr. Bright continued, "there are two very important questions concerning the Holy Spirit: First, why should a Christian want to be filled with the Holy Spirit? It is impossible to live a holy life and be a fruitful witness for our Lord apart from the Holy Spirit. It is the Holy Spirit who empowers the believer for a fruitful witness. Jesus said, 'You shall receive power when the Holy Spirit has come upon you; and you shall be My witnesses both in Jerusalem, and in all Judea and Samaria, and even to the remotest part of the earth' (Acts 1:8). It is not only impossible to become a Christian apart from the Holy Spirit; it is also impossible to produce the fruit of the Spirit in our lives (Gal. 5:22–23).

"Second, how can one be filled with the Holy Spirit? Suppose that you want to cash a check for a hundred dollars. Would you go to the bank where you have several thousand dollars on deposit, place the check on the counter, get down on your knees, and say, 'Oh, please, Mr. Teller, cash my check?' No, you would simply go in faith, place the check on the counter, and wait for the money which is already yours. Similarly, in asking God to fill us with His Holy Spirit, we are asking for what is already ours by right, as children of God.

"Though you are filled with the Holy Spirit by faith and faith alone, it is important to recognize that several factors contribute to preparing your heart for the filling of the Spirit.

"First, you must hunger and thirst after God and desire to be filled with the Spirit. We have the promise of our Savior, 'Blessed are those who hunger and thirst for righteousness, for they shall be satisfied' (Matt. 5:6).

"Second, be willing to surrender the direction and control of your life to Christ in accordance with Paul's admonition in Rom. 12:1, 2: 'And so, dear brothers, I plead with you to give your bodies to God. Let them be a living sacrifice, holy—the kind He can accept. When you think of what He has done for you, is this too much to ask? Don't copy the behavior and customs of this world, but be a new and different person with a fresh newness in all you do and think. Then you will learn from your own experience how His ways will satisfy you' (LB).

"Third, confess every known sin that the Holy Spirit brings to your remembrance and experience the cleansing and forgiveness that God promises in 1 John 1:9: 'But if we confess our sins to Him, He can be depended on to forgive us and to cleanse us from every wrong. And it is perfectly proper for God to do this for us because Christ died to wash away our sins' (LB).

"Two important words spell out the steps to being filled with the Spirit. The first is *command*. In Eph. 5:18, God commands us to be filled: 'Be not drunk with wine, in which is excess, but be filled with the Spirit' (KJV).

"The other word is *promise*—a promise that makes it possible to obey the command: 'And this is the confidence which we have before Him, that, if we ask anything according to His will, He hears us. And if we know that He hears us in whatever we ask, we know that we have the requests which we have asked from Him' (1 John 5:14–15).

"Now, Josh, as a Christian, you already have the Holy

Spirit dwelling within you. Therefore, you do not need to invite Him to come into your life. The moment you received Christ, the Holy Spirit not only came to indwell you, but He also imparted to you spiritual life, causing you to be born anew as a child of God. The Holy Spirit also baptized you into the body of Christ.

"There is just one indwelling of the Holy Spirit, one rebirth through the ministry of the Holy Spirit, and one baptism of the Holy Spirit—all of which occur the moment you receive Christ. There are many fillings, as is made clear in Eph. 5:18. In the Greek language this command of God, 'Be ye being filled,' means to keep constantly and continually being filled, controlled, and empowered with the Holy Spirit as a way of life.

"Josh," Dr. Bright probed, "have you met God's conditions for heart preparation? Do you hunger and thirst after righteousness? Have you confessed all known sin? Are you willing to demonstrate your faith by offering this or a similar prayer right now?"

Right then I prayed with Dr. Bright: "Dear Father, I need You. I acknowledge that I have been in control of my life and that, as a result, I have sinned against You. I thank You for forgiving my sins through Christ's death on the cross for me. I now invite Christ to take control of the throne of my life. Fill me with the Holy Spirit as You commanded me to be filled and as You promised in Your Word that You would do if I asked in faith. I pray this in the authority of the name of the Lord Jesus Christ. As an expression of my faith, I now thank You for filling me with Your Holy Spirit and for taking control of my life."

Then Dr. Bright confirmed God's promise. "Josh, you can be sure that God has answered you. You are now filled with the Holy Spirit whether you feel like it or not. Do not depend on emotions; we are to live by faith, not feelings, though feelings based on faith and obedience are valid, according to John 14:21."

Then Dr. Bright closed with a key thought: "Thank God each day for the fullness of His Spirit. This is your heritage as a child of God—a life of purpose, power, and fruitful witness that brings glory to our Savior. Remember, a day not lived in the fullness, power, and control of the Holy Spirit is a wasted day."

The promise of the indwelling presence of the Holy Spirit is for all of us to receive by faith. If you want it for your life, why don't you start by writing a prayer to God? Thank Him for providing His Holy Spirit to cleanse and empower your life. Then tell Him that you are trusting Him for the fullness of His Holy Spirit to pervade and control your life. Ask God to make His Holy Spirit's presence, understanding, and power in your life more evident to you. Then, daily, allow Him by faith to give you more and more of His enabling power.

In Christ you are adequate. You can accomplish all that God wants you to achieve and be. You can face life courageously and hopefully because of an expanding understanding and experience of being filled with God's Spirit. What a joy to experience having every need of our lives met by faith, resting on the solid foundation of our Lord and Savior, Jesus Christ.

Josh McDowell is an internationally known speaker, author and traveling representative of Campus Crusade for Christ. He has authored over 30 books including *Why Wait?, Love, Dad, How to Help You Child Say No to Sexual Pressure and The Secret of Loving.* A magna cum laude graduate of Talbot Theological Seminary and a member of two national honor societies, Josh lives with his wife, Dottie, and their four children.

Dr. Dale Bellis has pastored for 10 years and has co-authored five curriculum teaching programs with Josh McDowell. He received his Doctor of Ministry degree from Luther Rice Seminary and is a graduate of Columbia Graduate School in Columbia, South Carolina. Dale lives in Alliance, Ohio, with his wife, Brenda, and their three children.